MALTA

Paul the Apostle, statue on St Paul's Island, Selmunett, *c.* 1960. In AD 58, when Paul was a Roman citizen and himself a prisoner, he was sent by boat from Syria to Rome with other prisoners to appear for trial before the Emperor. According to the *Acts of the Apostles* and local Maltese tradition on the fourteenth night of the voyage the ship was caught in a storm in the Mediterranean and struck the rocky island called Melita in what is now known as St Paul's Bay. The prisoners swam ashore and local people lit a fire to warm them. It is said that a snake then came out of the fire and fastened itself to Paul's hand which the people took as a sign; they said, 'This man must be a murderer but Fate will not let him live though he escaped from the sea.' Paul, however, shook off the snake without being hurt, an act that changed the minds of the onlookers who then believed he was a god. They brought him the sick, including the father of Publius, the ruler of the island. Paul's preaching and acts of healing converted the island to Christianity and after several months he and the other prisoners resumed their journey to Rome. A statue 4 m high stands on a 8.3 m platform on the spot where Paul's vessel was shipwrecked. It was erected in 1845 and owing to its exposure to the elements the statue is now in constant need of renovation. It was fully restored in 1996 by Din l-Art Helwa.

OLD PHOTOGRAPHS OF

MALTA

CARMELINA GRECH

SUTTON PUBLISHING LIMITED

Sutton Publishing Limited
Phoenix Mill · Thrupp · Stroud
Gloucestershire · GL5 2BU

First published 1999

Cover photographs: *front cover*: Grand Harbour, *c.* 1896. *Back cover*: the fleet entering Grand Harbour during the First World War.
Half-title page: *British Warship in Valletta Harbour*, watercolour by Lieutenant Rudolph de Lisle RN, *c.* 1870.

Consultant: Trevor Hickman, Wymondham, Melton Mowbray, Leicestershire, UK.

British Library Cataloguing in Publication Data
A catalogue record for this book is available from the British Library.

ISBN 0-7509-2188-9

Typeset in 10/12 Perpetua.
Typesetting and origination by
Sutton Publishing Limited.
Printed in Great Britain by
Ebenezer Baylis, Worcester.

Distributed in Malta and Gozo by:
Progress Press Co. Ltd, 341 St Paul Street, Valletta, VLT07, MALTA.

Between 1833 and 1863 the Rotunda of Mosta was erected by voluntary labour on the site of the demolished Tommaso Dingli church. It was the brainchild of Giorgio Grognet de Vasse, a military engineer, who modelled the church on the Pantheon in Rome. The dome is reputedly the third largest unsupported structure of its kind in the world.

CONTENTS

Chalet-Għar id-dud, Sliema, *c.* 1930.

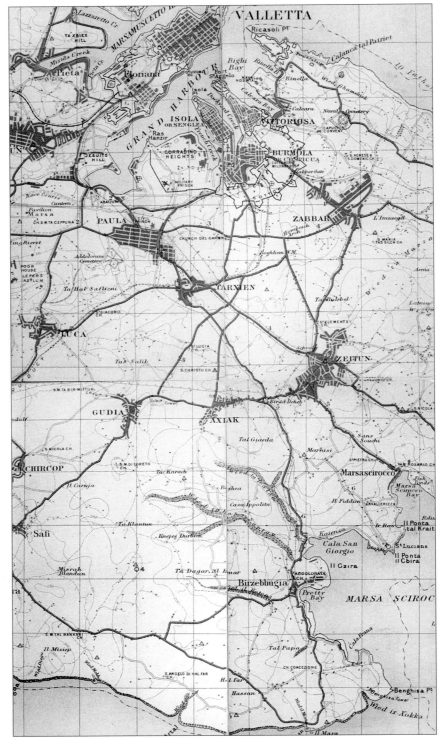

Section of a military map prepared by the British Army's Royal Engineers, 1910.

INTRODUCTION

T he first book that made a real impression on me was *Street of Adventure* by Philip Gibbs. I was twelve, and from that moment the seed of the desire to write was sown and began to put down deep roots. It lay dormant in a hidden corner for a long time but then, when I was fifty-one years old, the opportunity to let it grow and flourish finally came. I saw an advertisement for a two-year evening course in journalism at the University of Malta. Although it came at a difficult and perplexing time in my life, I decided to take the chance; I enrolled to sit on a lecture room bench with young students and learn the art of writing.

After two years, I was awarded a certificate of proficiency. Then it was time to obey the force inside me, take up my pen and write. It was Trevor Hickman who spurred me on to undertake this book and it gave me great satisfaction to dig through my accumulated excerpts and put them together for this collection. It is a happy feeling to realize that the material is finally being used.

The aim of this book is simple: to take an affectionate glance at the Malta of the past — its views, cultural values, entertainment and leisure, church and royalty, folklore and politics, war experiences, toil and survival. These pages record significant accomplishments blended with remarkable past events and the unique lifestyle and traditions of the island's people — traditions that are unfortunately disappearing into oblivion. I hope this book will brighten the reminiscences of the old but, most of all, that it will have some allure for the young and encourage them to cultivate an interest in and a respect for knowledge and the appreciation of our heritage.

The olive tree, *olea Europaea*, was once widely cultivated in the islands for the production of oil. This has been revealed by the number of oil presses discovered in ruined Roman farmhouses and by placenames like Zebbug (olives) and Ghasri (pressing). Olive trees have a long life and are still grown, although now the fruit is pickled for local consumption rather than pressed for oil.

DEDICATION

With the greatest love I dedicate this book to my five children, Edwina, Stefan, Bernard, Norman and Simon, their husband and wives and my (to date) ten grandchildren. They have all given me great help and encouragement in completing this book.

I would like to thank my friends who readily handed me their treasured family photos, especially Yvonne de Domenico who laid open her family albums that hold so many personal memories and entreated me to make my selection from the pictures. She was the pioneer who set my journey in motion. In researching this book I have met people from many different walks of life who were generous and a great asset to my work. I realized what little knowledge I possess and that our libraries are true seats of learning. I acknowledge with thanks everyone who listened patiently to my queries and obliged me with answers.

This book is a dream come true and one that I am delighted to share with my readers.

Carmelina Grech

The author's brother John Brincat, sister Mary and the author in Carnival dress, 1930.

The author's grandmother Carmela (1843–1933) and mother Vittoria (1890–1971), Ciancio.

HISTORICAL BACKGROUND

Malta has a long, interesting and eventful history. The first Maltese were late Stone Age farmers who migrated to the islands from Sicily some time before 4000 BC. Cave dwellings, stone circles and mysterious temples survive from the Palaeolithic and Neolithic periods, *c.* 5,000 BC, including the temples at Hal Tarxien and Hal Saflieni Hypogeum (*see* p. 12) that were used in the fourth and third millennia BC and are among the wonders of the world. The Neolithic people also built the megalithic temples of Hagar Qim (*see* p. 39) and Mnajdra, themselves invaluable treasures.

Some time in the eighth century BC, the sea-faring Phoenicians, then at the height of their power and prosperity, established themselves as a trading community in the Mediterranean. They invaded and colonized the Maltese Islands, built temples and introduced their own Semitic language.

In 550 BC, Malta was conquered by Carthage. The Carthaginians had much in common with the people of Malta and spoke a similar Semitic tongue. They were a great naval and trading race and succeeded in holding the islands until 216 BC when they were defeated by the Romans during the Second Punic War. Malta prospered under Roman rule; its people were treated well by the conquerors and eventually enjoyed a measure of autonomy. Today, remains of the Roman occupation centre around Rabat where temples, villas and baths testify to the presence of a cultured class and reveal the results of Maltese contact with Latin civilization. In AD 58 St Paul was shipwrecked on Malta and brought Christianity to the islands.

When the Roman empire was divided in 395 Malta fell under the jurisdiction of the eastern half, which was ruled from Byzantium, and when the empire eventually fell it was captured by the Arabs. In 870 they crossed from Sicily and thus started an occupation that was to last 220 years. The Arab people left a strong imprint on the culture and pattern of Maltese life as well as enriching the islands' language. Then, in 1090, Count Roger of Normandy launched an attack from Sicily and annexed Malta to his domain, bringing it back within the Christian orbit. It became an outpost of the Sicilian kingdom under Norman and French rule. In 1284 the French were defeated by a fleet from Aragon which by turns granted the Maltese islands to a number of feudal lords or brought them within the royal domain.

By the sixteenth century the Mediterranean had become the scene of struggles between the Cross and the Crescent. The main defenders of the Cross were the Knights of St John who fought for the Christian faith from their base in Rhodes until they were driven out by the Ottoman Sultan Suleiman. The Knights were then homeless and in 1530, through the intervention of the Pope, the Holy Roman Emperor Charles V gave Malta to the Order of St John for the annual tribute of one Maltese falcon.

The wrath of Suleiman was turned against the islands and in 1565 he sent a vast armada of nearly 200 ships carrying more than 30,000 fighting men to attack them. The knights were determined not to lose their new base so, under the leadership of Grand Master Jean Parisot de La Valette, and aided by the Maltese, they firmly resisted the onslaught. The women and children hurled rocks and flares – which started burning the Turks' voluminous tunics – and poured cauldrons of boiling water and tar upon their attackers. The defenders of St Elmo fought gallantly but were overwhelmed and brutally massacred. The Turks carved crosses on the breasts of their prisoners, crucified them, and floated their bodies across the Grand Harbour. The defenders retaliated by beheading their Turkish captives and using their heads as cannon balls.

However, the citadels of Birgu and Mdina held fast until the Turks eventually lost heart and withdrew to relief ships arriving from Sicily. The gallantry of the defenders had prevented the Turks attacking Western Europe. So much importance was given to the victory throughout Europe that even Queen Elizabeth of England ordered special prayers of intercession for the besieged, and later thanksgiving prayers for the Victory of Malta. Amid great rejoicing Birgu was renamed Vittoriosa. In the year following the siege the foundations were laid for the city of Valletta. This was built to be an impregnable bulwark against the Turks – Sir Walter Scott compared it to 'a dream', Disraeli styled it 'a city of Palaces' and Napoleon and Nelson both called it 'the greatest stronghold of Europe' – a city unparalleled in military architecture with its streets laid out in a grid pattern. A great centre of culture was created and there were many fine buildings including a palace for the Grand Master, auberges for the knights, a conventual church dedicated to St John, an imposing library and theatres, as well as hospitals and armouries. Great works of art were commissioned from artists like Caravaggio, Mattia Preti, Favray and others.

The conventual church of St John is the greatest creation of the famous Maltese architect Girolamo Cassar who converted the hill on which Valletta stands into a city of grandeur. The Knights of each 'Langue' or 'tongue' vied with one another in adorning and embellishing a chapel dedicated to their own language with monuments. The rich interior of St John's is a contrast to the austerity of its exterior; the vast nave with its sumptuous frescoes by the Calabrian painter Mattia Preti, the priceless altar pieces, the walls and mosaic slabs recording the achievements of distinguished dignitaries of the Order and emblazoned with the coats of arms of great princes, are exceptionally fine. The famous Flemish tapestries that are hung on special occasions were a gift from the Grand Master Perellos on his accession in 1697 and were manufactured by the renowned factory of Judecos de Vos, with designs by Rubens and Mattia Preti. Gobelins tapestries, a present from the same Grand Master, hang in the Tapestry Hall and are based on paintings donated by the Prince of Nassau to Louis XIV in 1679. The precious jewels of this cathedral are endless; it has an aura of splendour and is a symbol of the nation's faith.

In time with the growth of wealth and security, the Knights grew idle and arrogant, their martial spirit began to wane and the Maltese became dissatisfied with their rule. Ferdinand von Hompesch, a German Grand Master of weak character, capitulated to Napoleon Bonaparte in June 1798 when the French General requested permission for his fleet to enter the Grand Harbour and take on water on his way to Egypt. The Knights were forced to leave the island. Within six days Napoleon had laid down laws and plundered art treasures, including La Vallette's sword, which is now in the Louvre, Paris. After less than three months the Maltese revolted against the French garrison that Napoleon had left behind and confined within the fortifications of Valletta. Subsequently the islands were blockaded by the British fleet and French rule was brought to an abrupt close. Helped by Horatio Nelson, who – acting in the name of the King of the Two Sicilies – supplied the island with arms and men, the Maltese overthrew the French occupation and raised the British flag on the ramparts of Valletta in September 1800. The Treaty of Amiens in 1802 provided for the restoration of the islands to the Knights of St John. But, after insistent petition by the Maltese, the Treaty of Paris in 1814 ratified the cession already made by the 'Love of the Maltese', which laid down that the 'Island of Malta and its dependencies shall belong in full rights and sovereignty to His Britannic Majesty'. This phrase is engraved in bronze on marble over the Main Guard, Valletta.

Britain fully utilized the strategic position of the island and the history of British power in the Mediterranean is closely linked with Malta. Britain built a first-class dockyard in the Grand Harbour, concentrated her fleet in the harbour and was ready for duty if danger threatened the

Mediterranean. When the Suez Canal opened in 1869, the real importance of Malta became apparent: its position now lay on the main sea route between Britain and her eastern Empire. Steam was replacing sail on the seas and Malta became an important coaling and a transshipment port.

The years preceding the First World War were a period of constitutional evolution in Malta,and they also witnessed a series of controversies over the 'language question'. Until then the Maltese language had been a spoken but unwritten tongue. But a Maltese scholar, Mikiel Anton Vassalli, who had reduced the vernacular to a grammatical system, now became its first teacher. He had chaired a commission to revise courses at the University and it was on his insistence that the study of Maltese was introduced in the curriculum. This gave birth to the language that is written, studied and spoken today. But as it continued to develop internally, Malta was still attracting international attention. The Grand Harbour was the headquarters of the British Mediterranean Fleet and naval dockyards built by the British were a source of employment for thousands of workers and skilled craftsmen. Malta was not the scene of active fighting during the First World War but many Maltese served in the Royal Navy and the Merchant Navy. Other citizens rendered valuable service in the hospitals that were temporarily set up on the island to receive the wounded from the battlefields of Gallipoli and Salonika and the island was referred to as the 'Nurse of the Mediterranean'. As a recognition of her war effort, Malta was granted a form of self-government in May 1921.

During the first six years of the new constitution, power was in the hands of political groups that ultimately merged into the pro-Italian Nationalist Party. In 1927 the Nationalists were defeated by the Constitutional Party led by Sir Gerald Strickland. Disputes arose between the government and ecclesiastical authorities and when a general election was announced for the end of May 1930 the then Archbishop of Gozo intervened to forbid people to vote for the Constitutional Party. As a result, the Imperial government suspended the constitution. This drastic step added to the turmoil: the Italian propaganda machine took full advantage of the situation to stir up more trouble and the Nationalists made what capital they could out of the opposition of the church to Strickland's Constitutional Party. The situation was amicably settled when a British Royal Commission and an apostolic delegation arrived in Malta to act as peacemakers. The constitution was restored in 1932. The Italian government, however, continued to foster trouble in Malta and to support the pro-Italian faction in every possible way and the constitution was again suspended in November 1933. In 1939, shortly before the outbreak of the Second World War, a new constitution was introduced. This provided for a limited measure of home government but it did not come into force because of the outbreak of war.

During the Second World War, Malta was on the front line of the war in the Mediterranean. For months she stood alone, braving the might of Hitler's Luftwaffe and the *Regia Aeronautica*, an 'unsinkable aircraft carrier'. In April 1942, in recognition of her bravery, King George VI awarded the George Cross 'to the Island fortress of Malta, its people and defenders'. The British government re-established responsible government in 1947.

However, independence did not come until 20 September 1964. On this day Prince Philip presented the Instruments of Independence to Dr George Borg Olivier and at midnight on 21st the Maltese flag was hoisted to replace the Union Jack. Links with Britain remained strong and on 26 March 1972 Prime Minister Dom Mintoff and Lord Carrington signed the historic agreement at Marlborough House which enabled Britain to maintain her forces in Malta until 31 March 1979.

Finally, on 13 December 1974, Malta became a republic within the Commonwealth and the British Sovereign ceased to be the head of state, closing one chapter and opening another in the chequered history of a 'Fortress Island'.

HAL SAFLIENI HYPOGEUM

The accidental discovery in 1902 of the subterranean burial place at Hal Saflieni caused a sensation in world archaeological circles. The temple must have been carved into the rocks in about 3500 BC with simple tools made from flint and obsidian. It stands on a hilltop and consists of four sets of caves and galleries cut at different levels into the white limestone. The Hypogeum (the antechamber to the Holy of Holies is pictured left) is the most complex of Malta's prehistoric structures, a place of worship and an underground labyrinth with burial chambers and an echoing room where an oracle once made predictions of the future. The bones of over 7,000 people have been found at the site that could also have been used as a place for training priestesses. All traces of the mysterious people who built the Hypogeum disappeared in around 2000 BC at the height of the culture and their origin and fate remain unresolved questions. There are a number of other Stone Age temples in Malta and Gozo, erected during the fourth and third millennia BC. The earliest were built by piling huge rocks on top of each other, and the later temples at Hagar Qim were made of immense stones fitted together very closely to create smooth, regular forms. Some are extremely impressive – the seamless precision of Tarxien (*see* pillar niche, altar and spiral decorations, below), the huge megaliths of Ggantija and the refined architecture of Mnajdra. Equally strange and mysterious are the prehistoric tracks found on rocky ridges in Malta. The cut made by the tracks can be followed under water where the shoreline has subsided.

CHAPTER ONE

ARCHITECTURAL & SCENIC HERITAGE

An eighteenth-century engraving of the Auberge de Provence which was built in 1575 by Girolamo Cassar for the Knights of Provence. One of the first-floor rooms is richly decorated and has a wooden beamed roof with coffered panels. This wooden ceiling is protected by a pitched roof, one of the few in Malta. When the British military authorities occupied the islands they took over the auberge and used the top floor as the Malta Union Club. A musicians' gallery added to the hall hosted many colourful and festive occasions and was used as a dining room on a daily basis. Queen Elizabeth II and Prince Philip dined here. In 1958 the auberge became the National Museum.

VALLETTA

After the siege of 1565 Grand Master of the Order of St John, Fra Jean Parisot de La Vallette, realized the necessity of building a fortified capital city. He decided that Mount Sceberras, a ridge running out into a magnificent harbour, provided an excellent strategic position from which to command Fort St Elmo and Fort St Angelo and planned to build his city there. La Vallette asked Pope Pius V, head of the Order, for the services of his military engineers to help with the town planning. The Pope sent architect Francesco Laparelli, who was then in the employ of the Vatican State and an assistant of Michelangelo. Philip II of Spain also sent his own engineer, small changes were made to Laparelli's plan of the new city and it was named Valletta after its patron the Grand Master.

The first stone was laid on 28 March 1566. On the death of Laparelli, Girolamo Cassar was appointed architect in charge of designing the main buildings in Valletta. The Italian Grand Master Pietro del Monte sent Cassar to study the latest architectural styles in Rome. On his return he designed the Grand Master's palace, the seven auberges, the bakeries and windmills of Valletta but his greatest work is St John's cathedral, the conventual church of the Order. The exterior is mannerist in style, while the interior is early baroque with massive arches and ornate chapels dedicated to the patron saints of each Langue or tongue. The gilded decoration carved in the stone walls, the pavement inlaid with coloured marble and frescoed vault painted by Mattia Preti were added in the seventeenth century.

By 1582 Valletta was largely built up and by 1590 nearly 4,000 people were living in the new city. The Knights decreed that every corner building in the streets of Valletta must bear a holy statue and for outdoor life the city planners provided shady arcades in the main squares and leafy courtyards in all public buildings. Gardens were laid out on the bastions, Upper and Lower Barracca and The Mall. Alof de Wignacourt built an aqueduct to carry water from the springs of Rabat to Valletta and Floriana; the water line is marked by a buttressed tower with the arms of the Grand Master carved on it.

The main consideration in constructing the city was defence and this gave Valletta its unique character. As the danger of Turkish invasion receded, Cassar's austere façades were embellished with statuary and coats of arms. Then baroque additions were made in the eighteenth century.

Across the Grand Harbour from Valletta are the Three Cities of Senglea (Isla), Vittoriosa (Birgu), and further inland Cospicua (Bormla). The extreme tips of the harbour became the sites of two fortresses.

Fort St Angelo on Vittoriosa was constructed on the site of a pagan temple; under the Hohenstaufens in the thirteenth century a fort was erected that eventually evolved into a fortress in the days of the Knights. Under British rule it was the headquarters of the Commander-in-Chief of their fleet in the Mediterranean and became HMS *St Angelo*.

At the Valletta end of the Grand Harbour is Fort St Elmo. The first military construction on the site was probably a small tower built in 1488 and re-fortified in 1551. When the Ottoman Turkish invasion took place in 1565, the fort was the site of one of the most glorious, though tragic moments of Maltese military history. The Turks realized that in order to secure safe anchorage for their fleet in either of the two harbours flanking the peninsula, they had to defeat Fort St Elmo. After a massive attack on 23 June 1565 around 600 defenders of the fort battled to the last man. The badly damaged fort was rebuilt and called Upper St Elmo.

In 1687, in the reign of Grand Master Gregorio Caraffa, St Elmo's foreshore was enclosed with three new bastions. This corrected the inherent structural weakness of the star-shaped fort — its narrow pointed bastions provided inadequate gun platforms and could easily be battered by enemy gunfire. The new works on St Gregory's side facing Tigne Point are now known as Lower St Elmo and act as a powerful shield to Upper Fort St Elmo.

It was at this fort that Malta's involvement in the Second World War claimed its first victims in an Italian bombing raid on 12 June 1940. In July 1941 the fort was again centre-stage when its Maltese defenders proved instrumental in the repulsion of an Italian E-boat attack on a recently-arrived convoy in Grand Harbour.

Fort St Elmo's days of vigilance are now over. The upper part is used as a police academy and the lower part was the site for the shooting of the film *Midnight Express* (my children Edwina, Stefan and Bernard were extras).

An eighteenth-century engraving of the Auberge de Castille which was the seat of the Castilian and Portuguese knights of the Order of St John. It served as the headquarters of the British Army in Malta and today it houses the offices of the Prime Minister.

Porta Reale, seen here in about 1905, was erected in 1853 by the British to replace an older gate and was then demolished in 1964. The present City Gate was then built.

On a promontory opposite Fort St Elmo is Fort Ricasoli, named after the knight who paid for its construction. During the great siege of 1565 the site was occupied by Turkish troops attempting to break through the island's defence system. From the seventeenth century onwards the adjoining creek served as Malta's quarantines.

Fort St Michael was situated at the tip of Senglea. Now most of it has been dismantled, although a vedette, or guard post, still overlooks the harbour. The vedette features an eye and an ear in stone relief, symbolizing constant vigilance for enemy attacks. A number of these lookouts were constructed during the time of the Knights of Malta to serve as early warning posts for enemy attacks.

The Echaugette (see p. 63), popularly known as Il-Gardjola (the vedette), lies in the vicinity of St James Bastion. It is situated on the right side of the main Valletta gate and commands an excellent view of the Grand Harbour and the Three Cities and together with the Floriana area, Manoel Island promenade and Sliema/Ta'Xbiex front. The vedette suffered a number of unsympathetic changes over the years which gave it a dilapidated and generally bad appearance. It was restored by Din l-Art Helwa between the years 1995/6.

The forts themselves are bordered by inland creeks, providing shelter for ships in the Grand Harbour. Rinella Creek lies between Fort Riscasoli and the former Bighi Hospital — the residence in 1670 of a retired Grand Prior of Capua, Fra Giovanni Bighi, which, in the early 1830s, was officially designated a hospital for British sailors. Kalkara Creek runs on the other side of Bighi Hospital and was known as English Creek because it served as a berth for English shipping. Dockyard Creek between Vittoriosa and Senglea was strengthened by the Order of St John who constructed the Margherita Lines which provide defence for the inhabitants of Cospicua and its environs. The defence mechanism was eventually duplicated in the Cottonera Lines as protection against Turkish attack. French Creek was the site of the Royal Navy's repair docks and lies adjacent to the dockyard; these days the modern shipbuilding yard is beneath the Kordin Heights. At the furthest inland part of the Grand Harbour is Marsa Creek, which provides mooring and warehousing facilities for commercial shipping.

It was Grand Master del Monte who decided that the Order of St John should move to Valletta in 1571. On 18 March that year the Grand Master, the Order's Council and Knights heard mass in St Lawrence's church, Birgu, and then boarded galleys and sailed across the Grand Harbour singing the *Te Deum*. They processed to the church of Our Lady of Victory in Valletta, a fitting tribute to Malta's master builders.

The quay, Grand Harbour, 1916.

People arrive by tram at Porta Reale for celebrations to mark the coronation of King George V in 1911. On 23 February 1906 the tramway system was inaugurated and proved a huge success as public transport connected Valletta with all outlying districts. However, in the years that followed it suffered a series of setbacks and on 2 December 1929 Lord Strickland informed the Legislative Assembly of the tramway's insolvency; thirteen days later the service was terminated.

The façade of St John's cathedral, *c.* 1905.

St Lucia Street, Valletta, *c.* 1910.

The Sacra Infermeria, Valletta, 1918. On 7 November 1574 the Chapter General of the Order passed a resolution to construct an infirmary at Valletta and work started during the time of Grand Master Jean de la Cassier. The hospital contained six large wards with an altar in each. The Gran Sala was dedicated to the Holy Trinity and overlooked the Grand Harbour. It was the longest hall in Europe without pillars to support the roof. Structural additions were carried out in 1712 but were completely destroyed during the Second World War.

The hospital possessed an extensive library, which is now housed at the Public Library, and within the main quadrangle was a sundial probably made in 1774. In 1787 the Sacra Infermeria complex had a complement of 563 beds which could be increased to 914 in an emergency. It admitted male patients of every class (even slaves), as well as foreigners of every creed and nation; the hospital also had accommodation for illegitimate and destitute children.

The School of Anatomy and Surgery, later the Medical School of the University of Malta, was founded at the Infermeria in 1676 by Grand Master Nicola Cottonera. The hospital's proximity to the sea permitted the landing of the sick and wounded direct from the galleys to the seashore from whence a tunnel led directly to the wards.

During the French occupation, the Sacra Infermeria was used as a military hospital. It also served the British military forces as their garrison hospital from 1800 to 1920. During the First World War, thousands of British and Allied troops were treated for wounds suffered during the Dardanelles and Gallipoli campaigns. Surgeon (later Sir) David Bruce announced his important discovery of undulant fever – otherwise known as brucellosis – from this hospital in 1887.

The hospital was handed over to the civil government at the end of the First World War and functioned as the police headquarters until the outbreak of the Second World War when the building was evacuated. Four direct bomb hits caused massive damage. The part of the Long Ward left standing was used as an entertainment centre for the allied troops and became known as the Command Hall.

By 1951 it had been converted into a children's theatre known as the Knights' Hall and in 1959 became a school and examination hall. By the end of 1978 superb restoration work had transformed the complex to some of its former glory and the project won the Europa Nostra Award on 11 February 1979. Unfortunately fire swept through the building during preparations for a car launch on 25 March 1987 but it has now been rebuilt.

The beautiful edifices of the Strada Reale, Valletta, *c.* 1930. On the right is the imposing façade of the old Royal Opera House.

The Chapel of Bones, seen here in about 1908, was destroyed by bombing during the Second World War. Part of the cemetery of the Sacra Infermeria (*see* p. 18), it was built in 1612 by the Knight Fra Giorgio Nibbia and rebuilt in 1731. As this photograph shows, the interior was decorated with human bones.

Valletta and the entrance to the Grand Harbour, 1916.

The clock in the inner courtyard of the Grand Master's Palace was erected by Grand Master Pinto and has been keeping time since 22 June 1745. The clock is extremely ornate and has four dials: the one in the centre shows the hours and minutes; another above it registers the phases of the moon; the dial on the left shows the month; and the dial on the right indicates the date. Four bronze Moorish figures hold hammers that strike the gongs every fifteen minutes.

A view of the corner of St John's cathedral, showing the Red Cross Service Club, 1930s.

Customs House, *c.* 1920.

View of Valletta from Senglea, 1912.

A new era began just before the Second World War — railways and tram services succumbed to competition fro motorized transport.

Bus terminus. By the early 1930s both trains and trams were beaten by fierce competition from the bus services t developed into a network reaching every corner of the island. The tramway service ended on 15 December 1929. Villa bus routes were distinguished by the colour of the bus that made the journey — this created a colourful environment the terminus outside the City Gate.

FLORIANA

Floriana barracks, *c.* 1930.

St Publius church and the granaries, Floriana, *c.* 1930. The lids of the underground granaries can be seen in front of church. In the background is the round dome of Sarria church and opposite it is the neo-Gothic English church.

Activities were not disrupted by the repeated attacks from above during the Second World War. Workers are seen here filling sacks from the underground grain silos of Floriana. In the background is the partially destroyed church of St Publius.

MDINA

Mdina, also known as 'Citta Vecchia' and 'Citta Notabile', was the old capital of Malta and is one of the oldest towns in Europe. Its ancient title was Melita, from which the name of the whole island was derived. Standing on a high hill, it commands magnificent views of the island. Many of its buildings are a unique mix of medieval and baroque elements, not least because of the 1693 earthquake that devastated much of the city and made massive reconstruction necessary.

Mdina has a history stretching back nearly 3,000 years. In the early period it gained importance when Malta was conquered by the Romans. The remains of the influences of the people who inhabited the site during the Bronze Age and the Punic Period are today buried underground, except for a Roman pillar used as a bollard on the side of a building and two large stone blocks outside the courtyard walls of De Vilhena Palace. The city enjoyed considerable industrial and commercial prosperity as a Roman *municipium*. The Romans constructed heavy battlements and fortified gates, reducing the size of the city.

From the Arab civilization Mdina inherited architectural features and the tradition of building Maltese houses with flat roofs.

Mdina was sidelined in 1530 when, under the Knights of the Order of St John, the Grand Harbour area became the centre of activity and Vittoriosa the seat of power and authority. Mdina was the stronghold of the Maltese nobility who regarded the incursion of the Knights with suspicion and resentment, because they usurped the reins of control.

Some buildings may have been rebuilt, others repaired by patching the baroque style – so beloved by the Knights – on to the medieval structure. It is the imposing baroque style that stands out more than any other. The architectural heritage of Mdina creates a range of different impressions. The silence of the city is tangible in the narrow alleyways and streets that snake off the main square. Culture is also prominent. Palaces with their historic façades, doors and knockers are evidence of the ancient aristocracy, the gates and bastions are majestic defences and the churches are the treasures of Mdina, one of the foremost being its cathedral and adjoining museum.

The cathedral is one of the most ancient in Christendom, considerably enlarged and embellished between 1420 and 1679. It was almost completely rebuilt in 1697 – an architectural masterpiece by Lorenzo Gafa. There are paintings by Mattia Preti and a tall silver cross brought from Rhodes by the Knights, said to be the one carried into Jerusalem by Godfrey of Bouillon, the leader of the First Crusade.

The baroque Cathedral Museum is the proud keeper of the centuries of the islands' heritage in its vaults and corridors. The museum recalls the heyday of Maltese baroque art and combines exhibitions including architecture, paintings, sculpture and a unique collection of baroque music.

Grand Master Antonio Manoel de Vilhena girdled the baroque city with a new line of fortification. In 1724, as part of the new defences, the old main gate was moved to the west of its former site and the present one erected. In 1730 Vilhena built a Magisterial Palace on the site of the island's Comune Universitas. During the outbreak of the plague (1837) De Vilhena Palace was used as a temporary hospital and in 1858 as a hospital for eye diseases. It was subsequently turned into a sanatorium and inaugurated by King Edward VII as a hospital for the treatment of tuberculosis in 1909, becoming known as Connaught Hospital after the Duke of Connaught (Edward's brother). It ceased to be a hospital in 1956 and was turned into the Museum of Natural History.

The Norman House is another of the fine buildings in Mdina. Its title is a slight misnomer but is now in common usage. The house does not in fact date back to the Norman period and is only 500 years old – still old enough to deserve attention. It is one of the splendid buildings that pre-date the arrival of the Knights.

The fortifications of Mdina are one of its most impressive and enduring features, especially the vertical defensive walls near the city's main gate and at the northern end facing Mtarfa. Mdina was defended by four or five towers and one near the Greek Gate has survived. The gate was approached by a stone bridge over the outer *fossatum* that ended with a wooden drawbridge.

Mdina and its suburb Rabat are situated on high ground and approached by an interesting hill with its own historical background and architecture. The Saqqajja Fountain (above) was an important drinking fountain for the coach horses entering the city and is seen here in about 1930; others, less ornamental, also existed. The nobility held their council meetings in the elaborate building to the right that later served as a Casino Maltese.

Detail from a military map, c. 1910, showing the position of Rabat.

The Greek Gate (Porta dei Greci) at Notabile, probably so called because a Greek community had at one time inhabited the area.

RABAT

Rabat was a residential area long before Roman times. It has fascinating chapels with frescoes and ancient catacombs. St Agatha's and St Paul's catacombs are typical of the underground Christian cemeteries common in the fourth century AD. The characteristic feature of the Maltese catacombs is the presence of round tables: known as 'agape tables' they were hewn out of rock, with slanting sides on which mourners reclined in order to partake in a farewell repast.

St Paul's church is also renowned for St Paul's Grotto where it is said the saint lived during his three-month stay on the island after his shipwreck. There was considerable apprehension from the local populace when the Knights enriched this shrine and claimed authority over the city in the sixteenth century.

On the outskirts of Rabat are Howard Gardens and opposite the gardens is the Museum of Roman Antiquities, referred to as the Roman Villa. Several busts of the imperial family were found there, including a life-size portrait of a Julian Claudian princess, probably Antonia, the daughter of the Emperor Claudius. The *domus* was built in the traditional Roman fashion with an atrium floored in beautiful mosaic.

Beyond Rabat is Mtarfa, the site of the barracks of the British garrison and of Mtarfa Hospital, opened for British regiments and their families. Mtarfa was served by the train that started the long haul up to Rabat from Attard station; passengers would start buttoning up their overcoats in winter as the air became chillier the higher the train climbed. Rabat station was below street level and quite foreboding. Another tunnel, under Mdina, took passengers to the terminus at Museum station, so called because of the nearby Museum of Roman Antiquities. Here life took on a military aspect as most of the passengers on the train were the soldiers going to or coming from their barracks at Mtarfa.

Main entrance to Mdina, *c.* 1970, this photograph was taken from inside the city.

view of Citta Vecchia, early twentieth century.

oorway and knocker of the Casa Testaferrata, Mdina, Maltese craftsmanship of the highest order.

Two of the many balconies that enrich the narrow streets of the silent city of Mdina.

Doorway and knocker at the Inguanez Palace. The streets of Mdina are noted for their display of historic brass door knockers.

BIRGU

Birgu is one of Malta's oldest cities. Its location affords a natural safe anchorage in the sheltered creeks that run along its sides.

The Phoenicians were the first known settlers and reputedly erected a temple to Astarte. The Romans rededicated it to Juno. Then, when Islam started its march towards Europe and Malta was taken over, the Arabs constructed a fort on the high ridge to protect their vessels in the wharf. Subsequently the Normans built a chapel to Our Lady on the site of the pagan temple and within the fort. The Knights chose Birgu as the seat of the Order of St John and established their conventual church.

The church of St Lawrence, founded in 1090 at the same time as the Mdina cathedral, was at the centre of one of the earliest medieval parishes in Malta. After the fire of 1532 the Knights replaced the Norman church with a simple Renaissance edifice. It was the location for many important events including the investitures of Knights and Grand Masters. Here the *Te Deum* was solemnly sung in thanksgiving for the victory over the Turks. The Order's precious relics – the sacred icons of Our Lady of Filermos and Damascus – were venerated in St Lawrence's until their transfer to Valletta. In 1691 the present church was rebuilt to the design of the Maltese baroque architect Lorenzo Gafa. The enormous *pala d'altare* depicting the Martyrdom of St Lawrence is a masterly canvas executed by Mattia Preti; the ceiling paintings are by Cortis and Cali. Treasures salvaged from the bombing of the church in 1941 and 1942 are now in the Church Museum which has a number of other impressive old artefacts.

Birgu was renamed Vittoriosa after the Great Siege of 1565 and Victory Square is a historic reminder of the event. It contains the Victory Monument, built in 1705 and renovated in 1760, that shows Malta as a valorous lady in full battle armour; a hardstone crucifix that records the site of executions which took place before the sixteenth century; a statue of St Lawrence erected in 1880; the St Lawrence Band Club; and a granite stone bollard that used to mark the limits of the Collachio del Ordine – the area reserved for the private use of members of the Order. It is also the site of the medieval clock tower destroyed in 1942. Grand Master La Vallette addressed the Knights and the Maltese from here during the critical phase of the siege; originally it served as a lookout but was fitted with a clock in the seventeenth century.

THE AUBERGES

Birgu was the centre of all harbour activities; it had a class of wealthy traders and a community of sailors, port workers and maritime craftsmen. The Knights immediately started to construct administration buildings in the area and to provide auberges for the eight Langues of the Order.

The Auberge D'Allemagne was situated behind the bollard of the Collachio but was unfortunately destroyed during an air raid in 1942. A marble tablet denotes the site of the building.

The Auberge D'Angleterre encountered many difficulties as a result of the Reformation and the confiscation of the Langue's property in England in 1540. In spite of all efforts the English knights were unable to have their own auberge in the new city of Valletta in 1572, but the auberge in Birgu still stands in its original state.

The Auberge de France has a palatial façade with Maltese moulding, designed by the Italian architect Bartolomeo Menga. A special function of the French knights was to supervise the running of the Sacra Infermeria, and this auberge was in use until 1586.

Auberge de Castillé and Auberge de Portugal were partially destroyed during the Second World War. They are now quite insignificant and contrast sharply with the monumental Auberge de Castillé at Valletta.

Auberge d'Aragon, which was shared with another small Spanish province, that of Novara, has been destroyed by modern alterations. The Langue was responsible for supplies to the Sacra Infermeria and the troops.

Auberge d'Italie was the home of a large number of Knights from Italy. The Italian Langue was strongly represented in the Order and secured for its members the prestigious post of Captain General of the Fleet. Next to the auberge the Langue had its own hospital and a small chapel dedicated to St Catherine. None of these has survived. The first carnival revelry in Malta was promoted by the Italian contingent in 1535.

Birgu's fortifications are breached by gates. This is the Couvre Le Porte, built in 1722.

The Prince of Wales Band Club premises, Birgu.

The statue of St Dominic of Guzman by Giovanni Darmanin, the Festa, Birgu, 1995.

This photograph shows the area where the slave prison existed during the time of the Knights. Here it is being cleared in 1902/6. Slaves captured as prisoners of war were used as rowers for the Knights' galleys and during times of plague they became nurses. If they survived they were guaranteed their freedom. None did.

Part of the façade of the entrance to the prison, *c.* 1900. The building was once used as offices or quarters for the prison staff. Silos for storage of grain, centre foreground, were constructed in 1532.

Valletta Harbour, watercolour by Lieutenant Rudolph de Lisle RN. De Lisle was born in Leicestershire in 1853 to Ambrose and Laura Phillipps de Lisle. Although he was a Catholic at a time when few Catholic officers were admitted to the British Navy his great desire was to pursue a naval career. After training on the *Britannia*, he joined HMS *Bristol* and visited Malta in November 1868, staying barely three weeks. De Lisle came to the island at least five times on different ships. His last visit was on HMS *Alexandra*, the flagship of the Mediterranean Fleet, in January 1883. *Alexandra* sailed on to Port Said to relieve General Gordon who was besieged at Khartoum by the Mahdists. De Lisle was part of a hand-picked group under the leadership of Sir Herbert Stewart; as they were attacked by the Mahdists on 17 January 1883 their Gatling gun jammed and the whole contingent was killed. De Lisle was posthumously awarded the Sudan Medal with clasps for the Nile and Abu Klea.

Cospicua, the inner basin where number one dry dock was built in the early years of the nineteenth century. The domes and steeples of Cospicua parish church can be seen in the background and the dock is surrounded by workshops. In the foreground is a regatta boat.

Cannon fortifications at Birgu, the post defended by the French Knights. Vittoriosa's fortifications were defended at their separate posts by Knights of each Langue of the Order of St John.

View of the site of the Royal Engineers' offices, Vittoriosa, seen from Bighi foreshore, 20 January 1905.

EXAMPLES OF THE ISLAND'S HERITAGE

Sixty-two papal legates lived in succession at the Inquisitors' Palace between 1571 and 1798; twenty-four became cardinals, three bishops and two pontiffs. The chancellery walls were decorated with the coats of arms of the inquisitors. The palace had its own dungeons, prison cells, residential rooms, chapel and library. Similar places in Europe were suppressed and destroyed, and this palace is now of unique historical importance.

The Magisterial Palace was the home of the Grand Masters of St John, constructed soon after the Order's arrival in 1530. When they left for Valletta it was handed to Benedictine nuns but was totally destroyed during the Second World War.

The Bishop's Palace was built by Bishop Cubelles in 1542 and enlarged by Bishop Cagliares in about 1620. Because the Grand Masters refused to allow the bishops to move to Valletta, the Bishop's Palace remained in use for many years. St Lawrence's was the officiating church.

Bettina Palace was the residence of a Maltese noble family; Lady Bettina Testaferrata Dorell lived there. The family has been praised for many social contributions and activities in Malta over the centuries. In about 1842 the Sisters of St Joseph – a teaching order – were established and housed in this palace.

The Palace of the Universita' was built by Grand Master d'Homedes in 1538 to serve as the Universita' – a body entrusted with the procurement of essential commodities for local people. The institution owned six underground granaries (now covered up) and remained active until 1813 when the Universita' was abolished by the first British governor, Sir Thomas Maitland.

The Executioner's House was the residence let free of charge to the executioner maintained by the Order. Symbols of this abhorred official are still engraved across a window there.

The Sacra Infermeria was built soon after the arrival of the Knights and quickly won a reputation all over Europe. The hospital was always at the heart of the Order's activities and throughout the ages kept true to its origins in the Knights' role as hospitallers during the crusades. The architecture is early Renaissance in style. After the Knights moved to Valletta in 1604 the building was donated to the nuns of St Benedict, and still serves as their convent.

The fleet was the strong military arm of the Order and the harbour, at times called Porto delle Galere, was the centre of supply for this instrument of power. Many sixteenth-century buildings, rich in history, are located in this area.

The Scamp Palace, previously the residence of the Capitano Generale of the Fleet (Captain General of the Galleys), obtained its name from the British engineer who made structural alterations to the palace when it became the office of the British Admiralty in 1818. It was later turned into quarters for officers of ships under refit. The building was severely damaged during the Second World War.

The British naval bakery, constructed in 1840 occupied the site on the wharf of the old arsenal of the Order. The large palaces along the innermost part of the wharf were the hostels of the galley captains, and St Andrew's chapel and an Anglican chapel were also in this bustling area of the island. Other buildings along the wharf were used for supply and equipment storage and also housed the Order's financial administration offices.

Vittoriosa wharf was the cradle of the history of Birgu which itself served as the principal city port of Malta and had an ancient maritime tradition. The wharf was the Order's grand marina with its famous arsenals and various old buildings and palaces facing Dockyard Creek. The ship-repairing facilities expanded considerably over a 300-year period into nearby Cospicua and Senglea, developing into the present dry docks. The wharf – along which were berthed the galleys of the Order, including the Grand Master's flagship – played an important part during the 1565 siege. A temporary pontoon was laid across the creek in order to assist the defence of Fort St Michael at Senglea. At the northern edge a chain boom was installed connecting Fort St Angelo bastions with Senglea Point and preventing Turkish craft from entering the creek.

Spencer's Monument in Blata-l-Bajda, *c.* 1935. The obelisk, built in 1831 to a design by architect Giorgio Pullicino, was originally erected on Corradino Hill. It commemorates a distinguished British naval officer Captain the Honourable Sir Robert Cavendish Spencer (1791–1830), the second son of Earl Spencer. He was posted to the Mediterranean in 1815 and thus began a lifelong connection with Malta. Knighted in 1828, he returned to the island in command of the frigate *Madagascar*. During his Mediterranean service he became well known in social circles dominated by British Army and Navy officers, Maltese upper classes and nobility, and he entertained lavishly. Spencer died on 4 November 1830 on HMS *Madagascar*, off Alexandria. His body was embalmed and brought to Malta for a funeral with honours due to his rank, and was laid to rest on 12 December 1830 in Lower St Michael's Bastion, Valletta.

View of the Grand Harbour with Valletta in the background, seen from Senglea Point with the vedette on the corner of the bastion, *c.* 1935.

SENGLEA

View of Senglea from Cospicua showing a crane operating within the dockyard workshops. In the background can b
seen the Naval School and the clock tower of 1902. Cospicua is also known as Bormal and is the youngest of the Thre
Cities. In 1717 the plans were laid out on a grid pattern. The town was eventually built in 1848 on Porto delle Galera
the old name for Dockyard Creek. It nestles behind number one dock. The parish church is dedicated to th
Immaculate Conception and was originally built in 1584, enlarged in 1637 and finally consecrated in 1732. The feas
of the Immaculate Conception is celebrated on 8 December. At the top of Cospicua is a church dedicated to St Pau
that was built in 1741. It suffered the ravages of the Second World War and a monument to the fallen stands below th
Collegiate church.

An aerial view of the dry docks, an ex-naval dockyard, 1960.

Senglea waterfront in the 1930s.

Senglea, also known as L'Isla, was planned by Grand Master De La Sengle on a grid pattern encircled by bastions in 1551. During the epic siege of 1565, Grand Master La Valette conducted the defence of the island, the Order and the whole of Christendom against the might of the Ottoman Empire and in that siege, though repeatedly attacked by the Turkish hordes, Senglea resisted valiantly and as a result was bestowed with the distinction of 'Civitas Invicta' (the Unconquered City) by Grand Master La Valette. After the Knights were driven out of Malta by Napoleon Bonaparte, Senglea became part of the municipality made up of the area around the Grand Harbour that was enclosed within the bastions. The vedette on the tip of the bastion epitomizes the role of the fortifications around the harbour. The sentry box has various symbols of watchfulness sculptured in high relief, including an eye, an ear and the crane bird. The inscription in Latin assures the inhabitants of the harbour area that the tower stands guard against any hostile force that may attempt to approach Maltese shores.

During the British occupation, the Royal Navy extended the shipyard built by the Knights to the other side of the town. Though beneficial to Senglea at the outset, it later contributed to its destruction during the Second World War; the dockyard became the target in a series of air attacks and the city was practically razed to the ground. Most of the scars left by the war have now been healed.

The Sanctuary of Maria Bambina, dedicated to the Nativity of Our Lady, was built as a monument in commemoration of the victory over the Ottoman forces in 1565. The feast is celebrated every year on 8 September. The church was decorated with the title of a Collegiate church in 1786 and elevated to the status of basilica in 1921. It was destroyed during heavy air attacks on HMS *Illustrious* in 1941.

CASAL MILLIERI

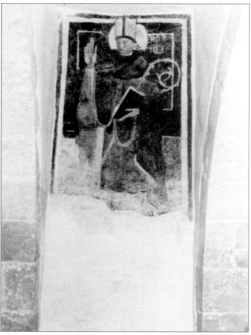

Casal Millieri is situated in the countryside between Zurrieq, Qrend
Mqabba and Kirkop. Although the village is first documented in 141
its origins are lost in antiquity and seep into Roman or perhaps eve
prehistoric times. In the sixteenth century the two small 'casali'
Hal Millieri and Hal Armanin shared a 'comestabulis' – a local offici
who represented them in the council of the Universita' at Mdina.

Two of the original four churches were pulled down and the othe
two were abandoned until 1968 when the Annunciation chapel – th
most important edifice of Hal Millieri, constructed in about 1480
was restored by Din l-Art Helwa (above).

The fifteenth-century building was constructed on the site of a
earlier chapel. Its exterior walls are of cut and faced stone blocks lai
in a regular formation. The interior is divided into five bays by pointe
arches arising from wall piers. With the exception of the apse, all wall
are covered with murals (left). The paintings that cover the walls of th
chapel are precious examples of fifteenth-century Maltese art an
seem to be in the Byzantinesque style of south-east Sicily; they wer
executed in the fresco technique between 1250 and 1550. Th
selection of saints depicted reinforces the supposition that they were
replica of the previous chapel's frescoes. The inscriptions are in ver
angular Gothic letters. Archaeological excavations brought to light th
flagstone floor, parts of the walls and half of the apse.

Hagar Qim, the largest of the Maltese megalithic temples, excavated between 1840 and 1893.

Hagar Qim stone tables and altars.

Hagar Qim standing stones.

GUDJA

The village of Gudja was called Bir Miftuh during the Middle Ages and its status as a parish was documented as early as 1436. The chapel of Santa Marija ta'Bir Miftuh is one of the few structures remaining from the medieval period in Malta. The Bir Miftuh building was one of the eight rural chapels which, together with Birgu and the cathedral, were included in the 1436 Rollo of Bishop Senatore de Melloi. Of the eight, only San Girgor in Zejtun and Bir Miftuh in Qrendi are still standing. It is recorded that the chapel originally had eight arches as opposed to the present six and was most probably in the shape of a cross with five chapels, including one that was rebuilt after the siege of 1565, and six side altars. By the late seventeenth century it had already been abandoned and was semi-derelict. Stones were taken from the collapsed walls for use in the building of the new Gudja church.

In April 1942 the Biz Miftuh Chapel was damaged by a bomb landing nearby and in the course of repairs the foundations of the original church were discovered. Over the main doors are the fragments of a very interesting fresco of the Last Judgment (below), dating from about 1480. The original work was composed in three or four tiers of figures: the first tier is dedicated to the Apostles and Mary, with the figure of Christ dominating the centre; the second tier held figures of angels, those to the right of Christ aiding the elect, those to the left castigating the damned. The entire right side of the fresco belonged by convention to the righteous while the left depicted the terror of Hell. The fresco was damaged and painted over when the 'naive style' fell from favour but it was rediscovered in the late twentieth century and restored to its present condition by Din l-Art Helwa.

The patron saint of the Gudja villagers is the Blessed Virgin of the Rosary and their devotion to this holy effigy is deeply rooted. A devotional congregation of Fratelli tar-Ruzarju (literally 'Brothers of the Rosary') was founded on 23 February 1588 when the parish was still called Bir Miftuh.

In 1919 Il-Fratellanza decided to institute a musical association and named it Circolo Musicale La Stella with the principal aim of setting up an orchestra to perform both in the church and in the village on Feast Day. In 1936 the orchestra was transformed into a band and kept the original name 'La Stella' (*see* p. 128). It plays an important role in the village feast that includes everything from colourful fireworks to brass bands.

t Roque chapel, Main Street, Zebbug. This was built in 1593 when the island was recovering from plague that claimed ,000 victims between May 1592 and October 1593. Mr Tomas Vassallo and his wife Katarina paid for its construction nd endowed it with revenue derived from a field on the Zebbug–Rabat road. The rent earned from the field was to pay or the singing of first vespers and mass on the feast of the patron saint on 16 August and for lighting the oil lamp on aturdays. Its interior is of a simple design with three arches and an altar made of local stone. It was inaugurated as a hrine commemorating the citizens of Zebbug who have contributed to the national culture in 1593.

Catacombs, Mqabba. The Christian tradition took over many f the tombs of the Roman period and extended many of them nto interconnected, labyrinthine catacombs, many of which till have the traces of frescos. An interesting characteristic of he catacombs is the 'agape' a round table partially surrounded y an inclined platform for guests to recline and eat a ommemorative meal.

Loreto church, Gudja.

San Anton Palace, Attard, a nineteenth-century engraving by Brockdorff. Built in 1620, San Anton Palace was originally the private country house and garden of the Provençal Knight of the Order of St John, Antoine de Paul, who became Grand Master in 1623. The palace had a formal garden, typical of the seventeenth century, which was built to give its owner recreation, relaxation, enjoyment and food – it was certainly not intended to be open to the public. Fountains and statues were part of the architecture of the garden; water was considered to add greatly to the enjoyment of the place. The planting pattern changed with the different tastes of the successive Grand Masters. The plan of San Anton was sent to Louis XIV of France to serve as a model for the garden of the Palace of Versailles. Napoleon's brother, the Prince of Canino, was later imprisoned here. With the advent of British rule, plants from faraway lands were brought to Malta and positioned close to the pathways at San Anton. The beds were filled with citrus trees – Queen Victoria received a special supply of oranges from the gardens every year. In 1882 Governor Sir Arthur Borton opened San Anton gardens to the public, creating Malta's first public gardens in which visiting heads of state, royalty and statesmen have since planted commemorative trees.

San Anton gardens, 1916.

The author at the eagle fountain, San Anton gardens, 1948. The fountain was designed by Grand Master Antoine de Paul so that gravity-fed water carried by lead pipes spouted from the two cherubs.

Attard, 1910.

The Fleur-de-Lys Gate, destroyed to make way for a British Services crane in the 1950s. The gate, erected by Grand Master Alof de Wignacourt in the seventeenth century, once formed part of the aqueduct that ran from the Mdina area to Valletta. The aqueduct had to cross the road when it reached Santa Venera. A gate in the form of a triumphal arch was built to camouflage the crossing. The artistically carved structure had three openings — a central one for horse-drawn vehicles and two outer ones for pedestrians.

MOSTA ROTUNDA

Mosta did not develop as a village until the late eighteenth century. At that time, owing to the rise in population, the old church could not accommodate all the worshippers and was pulled down. A new church was planned on the site but in 1830 a cholera epidemic broke out and the funds set aside for the church were used to control the disease and help victims.

When the situation returned to normal the scheme for the new church was revived and planning permission was obtained from the British authorities on 9 October 1832. The neo-classical design by George Grongnet de Vasse was accepted. (Grongnet was a local man descended from a family who had left France In 1685 after Louis XIV withdrew the edict granting freedom to French Protestants. The family included a number of important personalities including Rene Grongnet de Vasse, Grand Prior of the French Langue of the Order of St John, and Fra Angelo Grongnet, a conventual priest.) However, the parish priest, Joannes M. Schembri, opposed the plans, saying that they were too magnificent. He thought Gronget's proposed rotunda had pagan associations and favoured a cruciform design. Grongnet presented the technical details of the plans to a commission appointed by the Governor; it was approved with slight modifications, and the foundation stone was laid on 30 May 1833. The church was consecrated on 15 October 1871.

The Rotunda was the venue for the Eucharistic Congress that took place between 23 and 27 April 1913. Special papal legate Cardinal Domenico Ferrata lead the proceedings and was assisted by Cardinals Nava, Lualdi, Bourne and Santos. The Congress comprised a number of important orations on the liturgy of the Eucharist, delivered by various lay and ecclesiastical dignitaries, including a few from Malta itself. The British Forces provided half of the choir and the choirmaster. In commemoration of the event the street was renamed Via Congresso Eucharistico.

A dramatic moment in the church's history came in 1942 at the height of the Axis bombing of Malta when a 1000-kg bomb pierced the celebrated dome and landed on the floor in front of a congregation of 300. Miraculously it did not explode, no one was hurt by the falling masonry and only superficial damage was caused by the five other bombs that fell in the same raid. While the entire Rotunda had originally been built without resorting to any kind of scaffolding, the repair work demanded elaborate support for the workmen.

Near the church, to the south of Fort Mosta, is a family catacomb of the fourth to seventh centuries AD. It consists of a corridor flanked by two burial chambers on the left and another chamber and agape table on the right. The fact that there are two raised headrests and rounded depressions in each chamber indicates that each was intended to receive a husband and wife. The floor of the burial chambers on the left of the corridor is further hollowed to receive two more burials of small children. Close to the ditch on the south-east side of the fort is a Bronze Age silo cut into the surface of the rock, indicating that the area was part of a settlement.

Easter procession leaving the Mosta Rotunda, 1987.

A map of the area around Mosta showing the Victoria Lines to the north.

A soul in purgatory. The traveller in rural Malta will often see a stone image of a man or woman on a pedestal surrounded by flames. This is to remind him or her to pray for souls in purgatory.

The Rotunda dominating Mosta's farmland, c. 1890.

The iron bridge crossing Wied il-Ghasel (Valley of Honey), near Mosta, *c.* 1950. The bridge has long since been replaced by a more modern structure. A rough passage rises from the valley to Saint Paul the Hermit's chapel, picturesquely set high up in a cliff cave.

The author's sons, Mosta bridge valley, 1968. Left to right, Norman, Simon and Bernard Grech.

Naxxar parish church, dedicated to the Nativity of Our Lady, is a significant landmark, seen here in about 1950.

MSIDA

Msida developed from a small fishing and agricultural village into a flourishing community. The first recorded mention of the village was in 1535 when it had just a few farmhouses but the farmers, like those of St Julian's area, retired by sunset to Birkirkara which afforded them protection from the surprise raids of the corsairs. As the threat of attack receded, Msida's population grew, centred on the Valley Road and the area behind the church of the Immaculate Conception; later Rue D'Argens was named after Luca Boyer d'Argens, a French Knight of the Order of St John, who built a villa at the top of the hill.

Msida wharf served as a promenade for Valletta's inhabitants in summer and the village spread to include the area around L-Ghajn tal-Hasselin (Washerwomen Square). The place was first used for the treatment of cotton and hemp and then by women for doing their washing. It was covered over in the eighteenth century.

Transport from Valletta was by horse-drawn omnibus. Steam ferry boats were introduced in 1891, operating from two jetties with a service to St Julian's and Pieta Baths. Soon after, trams and motor transport were introduced.

Msida's first boys' primary school opened in 1856 with the girls' school admitting pupils the following year. Social life in the town comprised of civic committee clubs, theatres, the Boy Scouts movement, football, water polo and billiard teams. The Msida feast of St Joseph was initiated in 1892 and the greasy pole festival (*see* p. 107) was launched in July the same year.

The 'Parata' and 'Kukkanja' (maypole) began in the days of the Knights. The 'Parata' is rooted in the siege of 1565 and was performed in the Palace Square. Men dressed as Turks used wooden swords to fight others representing the Christian forces who finally lifted a girl dressed in a Maltese flag on their swords to signify the Christian victory.

The 'Kukkanja' consisted of a long pole covered with branches and ropes to which were attached items of food. A Maltese flag and a pigeon cage were hoisted to the top of the pole. Men climbed the pole to grab the food and as they did so were assailed by 'looters'. Their aim was to snatch the flag and set the pigeon free – in return for a reward.

Msida's main businesses were Casolani's stone saw-mill, Farrugia's furniture factory and the assembly of 'karozzin' and 'route bus'. Msida's main geographical feature is its valley which was once linked by a canal from L-Ghajn tal-Hasselin to the sea. Although the canal has been blocked off, a natural waterway still exists. Unfortunately this means that whenever it rains heavily, Msida is flooded by the streams flowing from Birkirkara and the Msida hills. This is a great inconvenience as well as a danger to local people.

A landmark in the history of Msida was the political meeting held on 5 October 1943 and addressed by Indri Cilia and Reggie Miller, which was instrumental in giving birth to the General Workers' Union.

Looking at one's reflection in Msida Bay is good for meditation, *c.* 1930.

The torpedo depot (centre) was used during the two world wars as a docking and a repair yard. It was leased to the Admiralty on 1 May 1855 on a 100-year lease for £40 per annum. It was also a submarine depot and was bombarded by Italy on 11 June 1940, the first day of that country's involvement in the Second World War. It later came under attack from the Luftwaffe.

Ta'Xbiex seafront with the quarantine harbour on the left and the two windmills that once dominated St Michael's bastions on the right. This 1858 engraving by Brockdorff shows elegant British military personnel and civilians on the Ta'Xbiex promenade. This was a high-class area that commanded a panoramic view. The land was owned by noble families and it is still held in high esteem. During the Second World War it was the target of some of the first enemy air raids, due to the presence of the anti-aircraft gun boat HMS Terror.

Msida on a normal day (above) and 'en fête' (below), before land was reclaimed from the sea. After the Second World War considerable alterations were made to the seafront at Msida, not least the filling in of a large area along the jetty that had previously been under water.

Rain causes havoc in Palma Square, Msida, *c.* 1960. The church parvis and the seafront experienced similar floods.

The rains came! Valley Road, Msida, was turned into a river. The Washerwomen Square – L-Ghajn tal-Hasselin – immersed in water (centre)!

On the right are the landings known as Sliema Ferries, c. 1930.

Sliema Ferries stretching into Tigne Bay, c. 1930.

The remains of the 'chalet' structure on the Ghar id-dud Promenade being battered by the fury of the winter waves (see page 5).

The Bonnici family, Senglea ferry landing place, *c.* 1930.

Tower Road, Sliema, *c.* 1935.

Spinola Palace, named after Grand Master Spinola, *c.* 1920. It once stood aloof watching over a few scattered boat houses and in the early twentieth century became a summer holiday resort for people from the city. During the First World War the palace served as the Pembroke Camp Hospital.

St Julian's, Kalkara Bay, *c.* 1950.

A shrine by a rainwater reservoir on the road to Girgenti.

The numerous niches containing effigies of saints or the Blessed Virgin testify to past religious fervour. Momentous events – like the passing of plague in a particular area – were commemorated by the building of a niche. The niches not only protect the statue from the elements but also allow the faithful to create little shrines by placing vases of flowers or lighted candles there. These shrines are often begun by individuals either in thanksgiving to a particular saint or in memory of a family member who may have died tragically.

Chapel at Girgenti.

ZEJTUN

Many olive trees were grown around Zejtun and oil was extracted from the fruit. Olive oil pressing was one of the most important trades in Malta's past. The earliest evidence of a settlement at Zejtun is from Punic and Roman times. The remains of a Roman farmhouse have been found near the village and even older signs of habitation have been unearthed in the area.

In 1797 Grand Master Ferdinand von Hompesch elevated the village to the status of town and called it Beland — his mother's maiden name.

A church dedicated to St Clement, and built to a design by Lorenzo Gafa, was started in 1692 and completed in 1720 on land donated by the aristocrat Girgor Bonici. The church was decorated with various ancient works of art and processional statues, including one of the titular saint that is still carried shoulder-high around the streets of Zejtun on Good Friday and during festas.

Country houses were built around Zejtun. Many have a central arched doorway leading to the house and a triple arched loggia or courtyard with a staircase leading to an upper storey with terraces. Palaces with large gardens and many other historic buildings also surround the village.

One of Zejtun's most interesting areas is Girgor Bonici Square, often called Cross Square because of the wooden cross on a stone plinth that dominates it. The cross was rescued from under the guns of French troops by the locals at the end of the eighteenth century and placed in the square as a sign of remembrance.

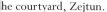
he courtyard, Zejtun.

The House of the Falconer, Zejtun.

Hompesch Arch, Zabbar. It was customary for people to ask the reigning Grand Master of the Order of St John to elevate their village to the status of a town so that they would gain prestige among their neighbours. Zabbar's inhabitants asked Grand Master Ferdinand von Hompesch to do just that for their village and by a decree it became Citta Hompesch on 14 September 1797. The event was commemorated with the building of this triumphal arch.

The Zabbar tragedy, 13 October 1975. When their RAF Vulcan bomber was ripped in three by two successive explosions in mid-air over Malta, the pilot and co-pilot miraculously survived. However, five crewmen lost their lives and Bice Zammit was burnt to death when a large chunk of wreckage fell on Sanctuary Street, Zabbar, and searing flames swept through it. Twenty civilians were hospitalized. The plane's fuselage, cockpit and a section of the undercarriage fell in a field called Tal-Qottu; debris was spread all over the area.

CHAPTER TWO

FORTRESS MALTA

The remains of a Bronze Age settlement on the exposed promontory, Borg-in Nadur.

The Neolithic people were peaceful and bequeathed to Malta a civilization rich with heritage. Their temple culture eventually came to a mysterious and abrupt end and the Bronze Age people, who were warriors, probably came from Sicily to Malta after it had been deserted. Bronze Age sites are situated in naturally defensible spots which are evidence of the insecurity and danger they faced on the Maltese Islands, perhaps from pirate raids. The most impressively fortified and defended Bronze Age settlement was Borg in-Nadur, the site of Il-Fawwara (*see* p. 57). It is splendidly situated on a small triangular promontory which juts out from the steep cliffs that bound the southern margin of the rocky plateau called the Gebel Ciantar. This period in Malta's history is still being researched but the other Bronze Age settlements that have already been discovered are all on the highest part of the high ground and consist of a massive wall with an enormous bulge forming a bastion in the centre.

The Romans built a town on the plateau on the site of what is now Mdina. Their successors, the Arabs, reduced the size of the town by digging a ditch on its landfront and surrounding it with strong ramparts. At the end of the Middle Ages the bastioned system of defence was developed as a result of the invention of bronze and cast-iron cannon balls that could damaged fortifications and thus demanded improved defences in response. The high walls of the medieval forts were designed to prevent scaling and the higher towers enabled the defenders to fire at the attackers. Walls became lower, thicker and more massive to withstand bombardment and were scarped in order to deflect cannon balls.

When the Knights of St John arrived in 1530 they began to employ the latest techniques to defend the island. Fort St Elmo was refortified in 1551/2 during the magistracy of Grand Master D'Homedes. Then, in order to relieve the fear of attack on the population in Birgu, Grand Master de la Sengle built walls and bastions to enclose the shore, leaving only the area of the Galley Creek open to allow the galleons to berth. He also founded a new fortified town on the peninsula and named it Senglea.

The fortifications of the Sceberras peninsula consisted of a bastioned landfront connected by lateral walls to Fort St Elmo. The landfront, sited on the highest point of the peninsula, was made up of two bastions and two demi-bastions. The original plan showed a total of three cavaliers but only two were built. They were to be separated from the mainland by a deep ditch. The bastions were cut from solid rock and very little masonry was used.

The construction of Valletta, begun in 1566, was the first link in an ever-expanding chain of defences encircling the harbour area and eventually extending to embrace the whole island. A number of coastal towers were built, some as lookouts and signalling posts, others to defend against an enemy landing. On the beaches a series of coastal entrenchments, batteries and redoubts were built and inland entrenchments designed to encounter enemy troops were constructed. In about 1610, during de Redin's grand mastership, thirteen or fourteen coastal towers were built, supplemented by stronger ones like Fort St Lucian, Fort St Thomas, Wignacourt Tower, Hamrija Tower, Ghallis Tower and so on. Then, in 1670 Fort Ricasoli was built opposite St Elmo to defend entry to the Grand Harbour and the defences of the harbours were strongly fortified by the completion of the Floriana fortification lines, the Santa Margherita and Cottonera schemes, the construction of the strong, well-built little fortress of Fort Manoel and Lazaretto and Tigne Fort on Dragut point at the entrance to the port. The Knights ensured that their fortifications kept abreast of modern developments abroad and engaged foreign experts on new projects, Italians being their first choice as architects and engineers. In the eighteenth century the French eclipsed the Italian engineers, and the Knights engaged the likes of Tigne, Mondion and Drummond Jervois.

Many centuries later, when Napoleon arrived in 1798, the technology of war and defence had developed even further. Fort St Angelo was one of the most powerful forts on the island, armed with some eighty guns and four mortars and garrisoned by a detachment from the Regiment of Malta under Knight de Hourney. But it was not enough. The surrender of Valletta and Floriana practically without a single shot and the conquest by Napoleon were far more than a military defeat; they marked the end of the Order of St John itself which no vulnerable fortress could have prevented. Napoleon, however, was impressed by the system of fortifications built up over the years. After the conquest, although offensive weapons developed, there was no real reappraisal of the fortifications for some time.

THE VICTORIA LINES

The Victoria Lines – a line of fortifications 12 km long, built between 1875 and 1885 under British rule – cut across Malta from Fomm ir-Rih to Bahar ic-Caghaq; that is, crossing from Pembroke in the east, through Swieqi, Ghargur, Naxxar, Mosta, St Paul's Bay, Rabat and Mgarr in the west. As technology of war and the threat of enemy landing developed, British engineers proposed the construction of a ring of defence around Valletta and the dockyard. Parts of the Great Fault Line used for defence in the Bronze Age and by the Knights were also fortified.

Four main forts were constructed and had a dual role, acting as both coastal defences against enemy ships and land-based artillery positions covering the approaches to the Victoria Lines. However, because of the topography of the island, there were still areas of dead ground along the coast, particularly in the north. So in addition to the forts, a continuous line of additional entrenchments with ditches was constructed for infantry defence along the whole length of the Victoria Lines in the years up to about 1902. Imtarfa barracks provided the troops.

The Victoria Lines were punctuated at intervals by heavy gun forts. Fort Madalena stood on the right of the escarpment – 400 feet above the sea. In 1873 the defence committee recommended the construction of the Battery at St George, renamed Fort Pembroke and completed in December 1879. An underground tank to hold 140,000 gallons of water was excavated to supply the garrison and the fort had accommodation for an officer and seventy rank-and-file troops. Targa Gap Battery, begun in 1878, is a classic example of an English hilltop fort. After years of disuse the casemated gun came back into popularity in the late nineteenth century but its revival was short lived. The battery was outdated as soon as it was built and armed. Gharghur Battery, a pentagonal work, was built on a site south of the village and armed with six high-angle 10-inch RML guns. In 1906 the removal of the guns was recommended unless they were required for land defence.

The Victoria Lines were constructed during the administration of His Excellency General Sir Arthur Lyon Freemantle and were named to commemorate the diamond jubilee of Queen Victoria. But geological faults weakened the defences and military exercises showed that the Victoria Lines could not offer a completely effective resistance against assault by a large landing force. In 1907 the defensive infantry role of the lines was abandoned in favour of the development of coastal defence.

arga Gap Battery, St Paul's Bay, c. 1960.

Victoria Lines approached from Bin Gemma, overlooking the centre of Malta.

Fort St Elmo, seen here in about 1960, a star-shaped fort like its sister construction Fort St Michael, was built in 1552 t
make two major contributions to the defence system. Firstly, it was to command the entrance to the Grand Harbou
where Fort St Angelo, the headquarters of the Order of St John, was situated. Secondly, it was to guard the entrance t
Marsamxetto Harbour.

St Thomas Tower, seen here in about 1960, was built on land purchased by reigning Grand Master Alof de Wignacou
and was completed in 1615. It guarded the entrance to Marsascala and St Thomas Bay while also acting as a lookout tow
for the remaining coastline. Signals were conveyed from its roof to other small towers on the coast. Under British ru
this fort continued to form part of the defence of the area, and during the Second World War it served as a detentic
camp for errant soldiers.

Torrii Mamo was built possibly in 1657 by the nobleman Gregory Mamo or his son George, who also constructed the wayside chapel of San Gaetano on land belonging to the family. The Mamo family erected the tower to withstand marauders and pirates who were a threat to the islands in the seventeenth century. Its shape – a St Andrew's cross with no fewer than sixteen sides – is unique in Maltese architecture and is seen here in about 1960. It was once surrounded by a ditch 2 m deep and was approached by a drawbridge. The ditch was cut into the rock and during the excavations a Punic tomb of the third century BC was discovered.

Wignacourt Tower, overlooking St Paul's Bay, was begun in 1609 and completed the following year. Quentin Hughes, in his book *Malta: a Guide to the Fortifications* (1993), described it as 'square in plan, it had a single, stone-vaulted room on the ground floor and another above. The flat roof mounted a cannon and had space for a bonfire, used for night signalling. . . . Four corner towers, unflanked, rose higher than the parapet on the roof and the main door was at first-floor level, approached over a drawbridge from a flight of stone steps. Originally there were drop boxes projecting from the corner of the towers from which objects could be dropped on to an attacker. As a result, this and its contemporary towers were called "towers of boiling water".'

Fort St Angelo, rich in military heritage, stands majestically at the tip of the promontory of Birgu. The Knights turned
into a formidable fortress against the repeated onslaughts of Muslim raiders. After 1912 the fort served as a shore
establishment for the Royal Navy and was called HMS *St Angelo* from 1933 until the departure of the British forces in
1979. The church of St Anne is inside the fort; the bulk of the structure is medieval but its central column is from a
Roman building and the side chapel was added by Grand Master L'Isle Adam in 1530.

Porta Reale, Valletta. This was designed by Tommaso Dingli in 1632 and pierces the bastions, *c*. 1930.

Upper Baracca balcony, Valletta, 1916.

The Ras il-Hamrija tower, on high cliffs at the edge of Qrendi. It was constructed in 1658 during the grand mastership of Martin de Redin and is one of thirteen coastal towers built to act as communication systems during enemy attack. These watch towers were not, however, capable of withstanding an onslaught by the corsairs. If the enemy was sighted during the day a red flag would be waved to indicate to Valletta that attack was imminent and at night a fire would be lit. De Redin died in February 1660 and with him died the enthusiasm for building coastal defences.

e late sixteenth-century vedette known as Il Gardjola the Echaugette) is similar to a number of others built strategic points on the landfront fortifications.

St Paul's convalescent camp was a temporary hospital at St Paul's Bay for the wounded of the First World War, a time when Malta was described as 'the Nurse of the Mediterranean'.

Mtarfa Military Hospital, *c.* 1930.

St Luke's Hospital (centre) under construction. On 5 April 1930 Sir John Du Cane, Governor of Malta, laid the foundation stone of the hospital which was described by the *Daily Maltese Chronicle* as 'the finest in Europe'.

A nineteenth-century engraving of Msida Bastion cemetery (Floriana Garden of Repose), used by the English as a burial ground until 1866. It is quite different from a twentieth-century Christian burial ground: old urns, sarcophagi, pillars, skull and crossbones and allegorical female figures veiling their sorrow predominate. It is the final resting place of several notable people from Malta's past including eighteenth-century English politician John Hookham Frere, Henry Pottinger (Hong Kong's first governor), Admiral Henry Hotham and Mikiel Anton Vassalli, father of the Maltese language. Many other names on the gravestones record British residents and visitors to the island.

The Turks' cemetery, 1917.

Above: Addolorata cemetery, *c.* 1930. Access to the cemetery was prohibited – except to priests and funeral cortèges – during the Second World War when the area was repeatedly hit by bombs. *Right*: The Barracca lift, operated by Macartney, McElroy & Co., which opened on 17 December 1905 and offered a lift service from the Customs House and the Grand Harbour area to the Upper Barracca gardens in Valletta, *c.* 1930.

A photograph taken from on board *The Star of Malta* as it entered the Grand Harbour on 8 September 1950. It was late sunk.

The *Maine*, photographed on 17 October 1943. The vessel had started life as a hospital ship funded by the ladies of Maine the United States during the Boer War when she was called the SS *Panama*. In 1921 the Royal Navy took her over and renamed her.

aval craft in Msida Bay where HMS *Forth* was berthed.

Grand Harbour, c. 1920. By 1897 – the year of Queen Victoria's diamond jubilee – the Mediterranean Fleet based
Malta had grown to ten battleships, nine cruisers, seven gun boats and fifteen destroyers. For further information on t
fleet see *Britain and Malta* by Joseph Attard (1988).

Between 1939 and 1945 the war headquarters were at Lascaris Bastions, Valletta. These fortifications, seen here in abc
1930, contained the offices of the Commander-in-Chief of the British Mediterranean Fleet.

Above: Dockyard Creek from Upper Barracca, showing Senglea in the background, *c*. 1930. *Right*: The names of the little bars along the narrow street in Valletta, which was called 'The Gut' by many generations of sailors, were meant to bring back memories of home.

A flotilla of destroyers in Sliema Creek, *c*. 1930.

SECOND WORLD WAR

Mussolini joined Hitler in the Second World War on Monday 10 June 1940. The first military casualties on Malta came the very next day at Fort St Elmo when six Royal Malta Artillerymen firing at an aircraft were killed by a bomb dropped among them. Gradually war became part of daily life. Bombs were dropped indiscriminately. Air-raid shelters were dug in the rocks and the old Valletta and Floriana railway tunnels were turned into temporary accommodation for refugees. Ancient catacombs were also converted into air-raid shelters. Malta's people went underground at the sound of the wailing of the alert siren and stayed until they heard the 'raiders passed' and subsequently the 'All Clear' signal.

An Information Bureau was established to publish regular bulletins – the first dated 23 July 1940 – with the aim of promoting anti-Italian feelings among the population, especially among the pro-Italian sympathizers. Malta's strategic position provided the British with an ideal base from which a strike force could operate against Italian targets. But the British aircraft carrier *Illustrious* itself became a target on 16 January 1941. The Luftwaffe swooped out of the sky and severely pounded the vessel as it was being repaired in French Creek. The *Illustrious* survived all efforts to sink her and limped into the harbour. But a further ordeal was yet to come. The enemy targeted the ship again from the air: it disappeared many times beneath the spray generated by near misses but did not sink. However, extensive damage was inflicted on property around the docks and the ancient places in Vittoriosa (Birgu) and Valletta (*see* p. 76) were reduced to ruins. No fewer than 100 aircraft, of which sixty were bombers, attacked Hal Far airfield.

On the evening of 24 March 1941 a formation of Junkers 88s escorted by Messerschmitt 109s dropped bombs in the Grand Harbour: Valletta was blitzed but miraculously Queen Victoria's statue survived (*see* p. 75). After the raid a number of unexploded enemy bombs were found in the city. The Junkers had also bombed airfields, rendering them unusable for some time. A quieter few months followed the raid but the lull was not to last. On Saturday 26 July a British communiqué read: 'Italian Light Forces consisting of E-Boats of various sizes attempted to breach the defences of Malta at about dawn. As has been customary throughout the war all the defences, many of which manned by local units, were ready and waiting for any form of attack. At 4.30 a.m. the searchlights were switched on and the battle began, during which a large explosion was heard in the vicinity of the breakwater viaduct near St Elmo. . . . It is very difficult to ascertain which boat fell to the shore defences, and which to the air, but no single boat escaped back to Sicily' (*see* p. 73).

The new year, 1942, brought intense and more frequent enemy attacks. In April the Axis unloaded 6,728 enemy bombs on the island but Malta's suffering was recognized. On 15th a message from the Secretary of State for the Colonies arrived. It read, 'I have it in command from the King to convey to you the following message: "To honour her brave people I award the George Cross to the Island Fortress of Malta to bear witness to a heroism and devotion that will long be famous in history".'

But this honour could not stem the effects of war. On 20 June the Lieutenant-Governor Sir Edward Jackson announced that food was in short supply. Bread was tightly rationed and a communal Victory Kitchen was set up (*see* p. 78). Other drastic cuts were made in supplies of petrol (which affected the bus service), sugar, edible oil, milk, fodder (which was made available only for horses used for transport) and the population of goats, sheep, cows and pigs was reduced. Relief did not come until mid-August when Malta rejoiced at the sight of a convoy that had made its way through mine-infested waters to the Grand Harbour. Among the relief ships was the US tanker *Ohio* which limped into harbour bringing fuel.

Malta's role now changed from defence to offence. RAF planes based on the island raided enemy airfields in Sicily and sank craft in the Mediterranean. In addition, merchant ships loaded with vital supplies now entered the harbour regularly. The Allies' fortunes were turning; with the victory of the Allied Forces in North Africa, church bells broke the silence that had been imposed since the outbreak of war. King George VI visited Malta on 20 June 1943 and was greeted by cheering crowds. Then, on 31 August, the Governor, broadcast the promise made by HM Government to restore to the people of Malta the kind of 'responsible government' they had enjoyed between 1921 and 1933. On 12 March 1944 the Sword of Honour was presented to Lord Gort in Zebbug. The inscription on it reads: 'Presented by the Band and Allied Clubs in Malta and Ghawdex, interpreters of the People's admiration, gratitude, devotion and love to H.E. Field Marshal the Viscount Gort, VC, their great leader and Governor during the Second Siege of Malta.' As war in Europe drew to a close, Winston Churchill said of the island, 'Malta is a little island with a great history. The record of the Maltese people throughout that long history is a record of constancy and fortitude.'

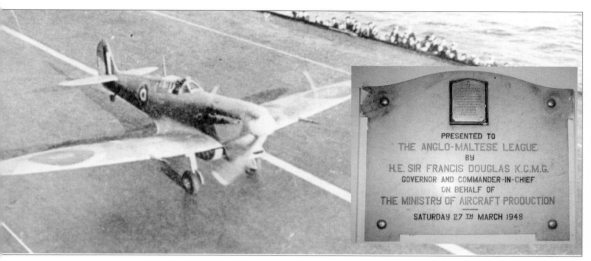

PRESENTED TO
THE ANGLO-MALTESE LEAGUE
BY
H.E. SIR FRANCIS DOUGLAS K.C.M.G.
GOVERNOR AND COMMANDER-IN-CHIEF
ON BEHALF OF
THE MINISTRY OF AIRCRAFT PRODUCTION
SATURDAY 27 TH MARCH 1948

A plaque at the entrance of the Anglo-Maltese League Club commemorates the two Spitfire 'Malta' and 'Ghawdex' presented by the people of Malta to the Ministry of Aircraft Production in November 1940. The raising of funds was but a minor facet in Malta's contribution to the war effort. The Anglo-Maltese League took the initiative and raised a 'Fighter Plane Fund' sponsored by Barclays Bank and Allied Newspapers Malta Ltd. In the first four days subscribers pledged £1,968 19s 5d and by the time the fund closed on 29 October there was sufficient money to build the two Spitfires. The inscription on the small brass plate above the plaque reads: 'In the hour of peril the Anglo-Maltese League earned the gratitude of the British Nations sustaining the valour of the Royal Air Force and fortifying the cause of freedom by the gift of Spitfire aircraft'. Lord Beaverbrook, Minister for Aircraft Production said: 'The gift that you have sent us will resound throughout the world to Malta's honour and glory.'

Fairey Albacores, torpedo bombers, c. 1941.

Milestones were defaced in many villages so that they would not help the enemy in the event of a successful invasion.

The one surviving Gladiator, 'Faith', was presented to Sir George Borg by Air Vice-Marshal Sir Keith Park in Palace Square on 3 September 1943, a year after the siege was broken.

The Information Bureau, set up in July 1940 after Italy joined the war.

A British heavy gun, part of the coastal defences on the alert, in the 1940s.

The breakwater footbridge, damaged by eight explosions in an attack by Italian E-boats on 26 July 1941. The Italians intended to force an entry to the Grand Harbour by destroying the span of the bridge but the debris blocked their way.

No. 3 Company, Royal Malta Artillery, on manoeuvres in 1913.

Gunners assembled in the courtyard of St Elmo to celebrate the Holy Mass marking the feast of St Barbara, the patron saint of artillery, 4 December 1953.

Queen Victoria's statue survives the bombing, March 1941. The statue was unveiled by Lady Smyth on 5 August 1891 in a ceremony attended by Sir Henry Smyth, Judge Pasquale Mifsud (chairman of the organizing committee) and Colonel Frederick Gatt (Aide de Camp to the Governor). The statue was designed by the Sicilian sculptor Giuseppe Valenti and the queen is depicted wearing a veil of Maltese lace.

An aerial view of the old town of Vittoriosa, including His Majesty's Victualling Yard, which was bombed during the Blitz.

Church of St Lawrence, Vittoriosa, 1942. German mines, bombs and torpedoes razed the chapter hall and the vestry to the ground.

Blitz-battered Auberge de France, the author's secondary school, Valletta, 1942.

Bombed crucifix oratory, Senglea, mid-January 1941.

'Valletta' by Judge Maurice Caruana Curran, published in *The Times of Malta*, Saturday 28 March 1942:

> Not for the princely monuments that form
> Our ancient heritage we weep today,
> Their very stones cry out above the storm
> That they shall rise again in proud array.
> Nor for the blood of slaughtered innocents
> Seek we revenge. They need it not who go
> To rest in halls of bannered firmaments
> With those who fought at Birgu and Lepanto.
> Valletta! We learn from you the ways
> Of dignity. Each token of your power
> Steels our breasts for more embattled days.
> We take our fate grim-lipped and cannot cower
> Who matin and vesper see the sun's warm rays
> Catch in their net of rose bastion and tower.

As the bombs fell, so the craters were filled. This photograph was taken on a Maltese airfield, c. 1941.

Balloons acted as a defence, c. 1940. Enemy planes got entangled in the wires that tethered the balloons to the ground. Here people are inspecting a balloon that was part of an exhibition of weapons held on the parvis of the Auberge de Castille to boost local morale.

Queuing for bread, Valletta, April 1942. Bread was rationed to approximately 12 oz per person per day.

Queuing for meals outside a communal Victory Kitchen, Valletta, 1942. The feeding scheme pooled scarce rations tha
were then cooked in one place, ensuring everyone had one hot meal a day. People were issued with a coupon to exchange
for the meal and abuse of the system was punished by imprisonment. Victory Kitchens were closed on 21 September 1943.

Barbara's Skew Arch at the Sa Maisons gardens (Tal-Milorda). The arch, designed by Maltese architect Giovanni Barbara, links two bastions. It was damaged during the Second World War and shrapnel holes can still be seen on both its sides.

Above: A pillbox, a British military outpost during the Second World War. In the background is the Selmun Palace.
Left: Night raid over Malta.

The disabled aircraft carrier HMS *Illustrious*, immobile in French Creek as enemy bombs fall around it, 10 January 1941.

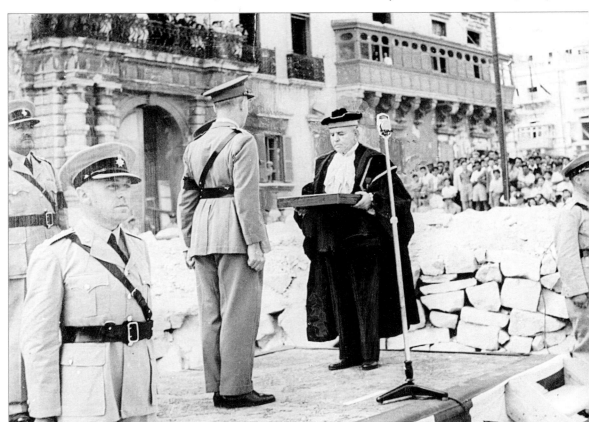

Malta is presented with the George Cross for gallantry, Palace Square, Valletta, 13 September 1942. Sir George Borg Chief Justice (right), receives the medal and citation from Governor Lord Gort. On the left are Police Commissione John Axisa and Superintendent George Cachia. Lining the square are representatives of the armed forces, the Specia Constabulary and the ARP (Air Raid Precautions).

A gun salute from above the Grand Harbour coordinated by wireless with the Royal Navy on HM Queen Mary, the Queen Mother's birthday, 27 May 1949.

Princess Elizabeth leaves Malta for Greece, 4 December 1950. The guard of honour was provided by the 1st Coast Regiment of the Royal Malta Artillery under Major G.C. Gatt.

ST ANDREW'S

The area of St Andrew's includes Swieqi, Ta'L-Ibrag and Madliena. It gained its name when Malta was a colony of the British Crown. The name Swieqi is probably derived from 'saqwi', which means fertile and well-watered soil. It is situated on a hill overlooking the beautiful valley of Wied il-Ghomor which separates Swieqi and L-Ibragg from San Gwann and tal-Mensija. St Rita's chapel at Swieqi was administered by an Augustinian community and catered for the spiritual needs of the few people who lived nearby. A woman called Marianne told the author that in the early 1950s there were only thirty families in the area.

Madliena owes its origin to the fifteenth-century chapel of St Mary Magdalen. In 1880 Fort Madliena was built on the site of the chapel at a time when British engineers working to plans by William Drummond Jervois were building pairs of forts facing each other across the Grand Harbour. Fort Madliena was one of four designed to strengthen the Victoria Lines of fortification that ran along the high escarpment from coast to coast.

The Pembroke barracks were built for the garrison and include large porticos built to offer shade; they have been described as 'a happy marriage between Victorian and vernacular architecture'. The barracks also had stables and workshops, and shooting ranges were set up nearby. This flat, rugged terrain was ideal for British weapons training and the ranges were often visited by high-ranking officers.

During the Second World War German prisoners were held at Pembroke barracks. No local person was allowed within 50 yards of the perimeter.

When they were off duty the British soldiers went to Jessie's Bar – the oldest in St Andrew's – which was owned by the Bezzina family. Marianne served drinks while her mother Theresa, better known as Jessie, cooked breakfast for the soldiers. Jessie's husband Saviour was the gardener at Pembroke cemetery.

Many beautiful houses and villas were built in the area during the late 1960s.

Father Stephen Borg donated land for the building of a church in St Andrew's. On 13 February 1966 Archbishop Gon blessed the foundation stone of the Maria Immakulata Omm tal-Knisja in the presence of Father Stephen and oth dignitaries; the church was given a title by the Vatican Council II.

The British military chapel at Pembroke, *c.* 1945. The area was used as a prisoner of war camp for German troops during the Second World War.

Boys Victor, Charles and Emmanuel Sammut with an official from the Pembroke target shooting range and an unknown man, 1960. The butts erected by the British forces for training still exist across the wild acres of the rocky beach at Pembroke, in ring a haven for exotic Mediterranean wild flowers.

An American soldier with a target, 1960s.

A new page was turned in Malta's history when the Honourable Dom Mintoff, Prime Minister of the Republic of Malta, lit the eternal flame of peace on Freedom Hill, Vittoriosa, 31 March 1979. Act LVIII was enacted by Parliament on 13 December 1974, making several changes to the constitution of the Commonwealth of Malta. On the same day Malta became a democratic republic within the British Commonwealth, founded on the principles of work and respect for the fundamental rights of the individual. The office of President of Malta was also established to replace that of the British Governor-General and thus the previous system of government was abolished. From that date executive authority has been vested in and exercised by the new President who is appointed by a resolution of the House of Representatives every five years. The first Maltese-born Governor, Sir Anthony Mamo QC, was nominated as the Republic's first President in 1974.

On 31 March 1979 the last British soldier left Malta, which was no longer a fortress serving the interests of foreign powers. A new chapter began in the history of the Maltese nation.

CHAPTER THREE

PASTIMES, PEOPLE & PERSONALITIES

First day cover to commemorate Princess Elizabeth's stay in Malta, 1950. Three postage stamps were issued — 1d green, 3d blue and 1s black.

Traditional pastimes on Malta are, not surprisingly, all connected with the sea — fishing, boating, swimming — and, during the Great Siege of 1565, what had previously been merely a pleasure became a valuable aid to the island's defence. Many heroes laid chains underwater to defend the forts and also carried secret messages by sea when it was dangerous to do so by land.

The mild climate encourages great enthusiasm for a variety of outdoor sports: football is forever gaining ground, tennis was always popular and traditional bareback horse races were run through the streets. The Order of St John helped to establish horse-racing as a favourite pastime and some of the races instituted during the time of the knights still survive.

The countryside offered hunters and bird-ringers ideal ground on which to indulge their hobby. But the beauty of the valleys and the high ridges also attracted artists and daytrippers from the towns.

In the villages people enthusiastically joined the theatre groups, local band clubs and the church parvis. For the more intellectual there were opera houses and many social events.

Malta has produced many scholars as our ancient National Library and notarial archives testify. The Maltese nobility is of great antiquity and the aristocracy's rights were recognized by the Knights and by the authorities during the period of British sovereignty. The distinctive institutions of the Maltese Church and State have also contributed a remarkable inheritance.

Ecclesiastical delegations, distinguished authors and political figures, Royal Commissions and royalty have all visited our islands and praised Malta and its people.

All dressed up for a special occasion, early twentieth century.

ward Vincenti and his wife Carmelina with relatives on a tour to St Paul's Bay in their Chevrolet, 1935.

nowned photographer Antonio Serracino Inglott took this picture of his family in a vintage car.

Juliet and Ethel Muscat with a friend enjoying their Sunday outing in their family's Ford.

Riding sidecar around St Paul's Bay in the 1920s was great fun! Yvonne Muscat is riding the motor cycle and her frie
are in the sidecar.

Y *Scaramouch*, owned by Joseph Muscat, berthed opposite his villa in Sliema Creek. Mr Muscat bought the yacht in
nt, England, in 1936 and sailed it to Malta.

Sammut heading out to go fishing at Marsascala, *c.* 1960. The small fishing village of Marsascala (or Wied il-Ghajn)
l had a very small population at the end of the nineteenth century. Its mid-seventeenth-century St Gajetan chapel was
important landmark for sailors who decorated the façade with graffiti, a sign that they turned to their patron saint
en in trouble. The Bidni chapel on the outskirts of the village was also a shrine for seafarers. There is an interesting
historic dolmen (megalithic tomb) in the area.

A political meeting at Marsascala, 1961.

A picnic gathering at Boschetto gardens, *c*. 1935. The history of the woodland gardens can be traced back to the time of Grand Master La Vallette who had a hunting lodge in the area in the 1560s. In 1586 Grand Master Verdalle built a castle on a rocky outcrop overlooking the fertile valley. Some fifty years passed before the woodland garden, linking the castle to La Vallette's lodge, was created. 'Buskett' was out of bounds to the Maltese people except on St John's feast day. In 1799 Verdala Palace was used to hold French prisoners of war, and was then left empty until 1851 when Governor Sir William Reid restored part of it for his own personal use. It is now the summer residence of Malta's president and the gardens are open to the public.

avid Russell (far right), manager of British Airways,
d Mrs Russell greet the Prime Minister Dr George
rg Olivier at their residence, Villa Florimont, in
Julian's. Dr Olivier (1911–79) was leader of the
ationalist Party and a respected statesman. At the
nited Nations his proposal for a Law of the Sea
ceived universal praise and approval. In 1950 he
came Prime Minister on the death of Dr E. Mizzi;
was thirty-nine and served as the youngest prime
nister in the Commonwealth from 1962 to 1971.
resigned as leader of the Nationalist Party in 1977
d died on 29 October 1979.

etching in the valley that runs from Museum station, Rabat, to Mtarfa. Here, an art class is led by Professor Edward
ruana Dingli from the Malta School of Arts.

A group photograph after a tennis match, Guardamangia, *c.* 1935.

Saviour Bonnici sitting in his stone hide enjoying an early morning hunt for birds.

The water polo team at St Julian's Bay with Spinola Palace in the background, 30 August 1919.

elegant mood — left to right, Carmelina Vincenti, Agnes
d Yioli, with Prince the black Pomeranian, c. 1925.

Yvonne de Domenico and relatives in one of the summerhouses
which once stood at the water's edge of Tigne, Sliema, c. 1935.

St Aloysius College students on a picnic, *c.* 1930.

Msida boys' school staff, photographed by Miss Eleonora Bartolo on 14 October 1910. Her father Augustu Bartolo sitting on the extreme right.

Left: Altar boy Edward Grech, December 1939. On Christmas Eve children participate in the Midnight Mass procession, carrying the figure of the baby Jesus around the church before the Christmas ceremonies begin. The highlight of the Mass is the sermon on the nativity delivered from the pulpit by an altar boy. *Above*: Votive processions were once common. This one was held on the feast of San Girgor, the first Wednesday following Easter, and used to travel from Mdina to Zejtun. After it finished people would flock to Marsaxlokk for the first swim of the year. *Below*: the latter tradition continues today.

Shoeshiner at work in the Upper Baracca gardens, Valletta, 1930s. A row of arches in the gardens leads to an open terrace that commands spectacular views of the Grand Harbour. The gardens contain monuments commemorating important events in Malta's history.

San Gwann Friendly Football Club after their cup final win against Santa Fe Oil Co., 1980. Back row, left to right: Charles Borg, Paul Mamo, Norman Grech, Alfred Mamo, Bernard Grech. Front row: Stefan Grech, Victor Sultana, Martin Sammit.

Mary and Charles Summit, 1948. In the background is Chalet-Ghar-id-dud.

Edwina Grech watching over her brother Stefan, 1957.

Joseph Brincat on a school holiday, Barracca, c. 1935.

Saviour Bonnici, enjoying his retirement, and caring for plants at his house in Birzebbugia, c. 1960.

Irene Revell's great-grandmother with her grandmother
(Paula Sammut) in her first Holy Communion dress.

Willie Guillaumier and family, Msida, c. 1910.

Maria and her sister Sunta Farragia, Msida, c. 1905.

Gladys by Sliema Creek. Parasols were all the
rage in the early twentieth century.

A mixed English and Maltese rowing crew, winners of the Regatta Shield, part of the National Day celebrations held on 8 September. Edward Vincenti is on the left at the front.

Left: Giuseppe Farrugia, brother of Publio, who enlisted in the Navy to see the world but was caught up in the First World War. *Right*: Publio Farrugia (left) and a friend. Publio was reported missing at the battle of Verdun in 1916. The following year Publio's mother received the medal which he was posthumously awarded. The citation read, 'He died for freedom and honour'.

Mediterranean Fever Commission, 1905. Dr Themistocles Zammit (back row, left) was part of the commission under the chairmanship of Sir David Bruce (front row, centre) who discovered that potentially fatal undulant fever was passed on to humans through animals' milk. This breakthrough was a remarkable step forward in fighting the disease, now better known as brucellosis. The spread of fever was brought under control by boiling milk before it was consumed and later (1938) by pasteurization: both procedures killed the bacteria responsible for the illness.

Sir Themistocles Zammit, the eminent bacteriologist, archaeologist, writer and historian, at work in his laboratory. He was made a CMG (Companion of St Michael and St George) in 1911 and created a Knight Bachelor in 1930.

Delegates arriving for the Eucharistic Congress, Mosta church, 1913 (*see also* p. 130).

The arrival of the Royal Commission, 1931. This body of people was appointed to mediate in the dispute between Lord Strickland, head of the government, and the Constitutional Party. The disagreement threatened to disrupt the impending general election.

Presentation of the Prince of Wales banner to the Prince of Wales' Own Band by His Excellency General Sir Charles Mansfield-Clarke GCB, GCVO, 26 December 1903. The Prince of Wales, later Edward VII (1841–1910), was the eldest son of Queen Victoria and Prince Albert. He undertook military training and was promoted to the rank of general in 1862.

The laying of the foundation stone for Duke of York Avenue, Valletta, 1927. This event was the highlight of a visit by the Duke of York (later George VI). He arrived with the Duchess on 17 June 1927; the royal couple stopped in Malta on their way back from Australia on HMS *Renown*. The foundation stone was inscribed with gilt lettering and contained coins and a commemorative parchment. It was blessed by Monsignor Michael Gonzi.

Queen Mary at the Hypogeum, 25 January 1912.

The Prince of Wales, later Edward VIII, presents the standard to Dr S. Vella, President of the Prince of Wales' Own Band, at Floriana, 2 November 1921.

Chief Justice Emeritus Carmelo Schembri (1922–97). Dr Schembri became Chief Justice and President of the Constitutional Court and the Court of Appeal in 1981. He was elected to the Legislative Assembly in 1950 and served as Deputy Speaker. He was Minister of Education in 1952/3 and was appointed Assistant Crown Counsel and Advocate of the Poor of Gozo in 1954.

Dr Paul Boffa (1890–1962) with the Duke and Duchess of Gloucester in the courtyard of the Palace, Valletta, November 1947. Boffa became leader of the Labour Party in 1927 and the islands' first Labour Prime Minister under the MacMichael Constitution of 1947. He was instrumental in replacing Italian with Maltese as the language of the law courts and was awarded the OBE in 1941.

Queen Elizabeth II and Prince Philip are welcomed to Parliament House by Prime Minister Dr George Borg Olivier on the occasion of the opening of Parliament, 15 November 1967. The Speaker, Dr Alfred Bonnici, is on the left.

In April 1921 Prince George, the fourth and youngest surviving son of George V and Queen Mary, was in Malta when Crown Prince Hirohito of Japan was also visiting. A census happened to be conducted at the time and both the princes appear in it.

Sir Francis Chichester on a visit to the island to view the yacht *The Mary Deare* owned by author Hammond Innes, March 1972. He is seen here with Brian Wilkes, the manager of the boat yard where the yacht was moored.

Chevalier Alexander Chetcuti MBE, the founder of the Anglo-Maltese League in 1935.

A mass meeting at Casal Pawla called by Dom Mintoff, leader of the Labour Party, during the election campaign of 1961
Dominic Mintoff was born in Cospicua in 1916. He graduated from the University of Malta, won a Rhodes Scholarship i
1939 and then graduated with an MA from the University of Oxford. He was secretary of the Malta Labour Party in 193
and between 1944 and 1947; a delegate to the National Assembly 1945–7; elected member of the Council c
Government 1945/6; member of the Legislative Assembly 1947–54; and Minister of Works and Reconstruction 1947–9
In 1949 Dom Mintoff disagreed with Dr P. Boffa – leader of the Malta Labour Party – about negotiations with Britai
involving marshal aid and the dismissal of redundant dockyard workers. The Labour Party was divided over this questio
but members elected Mintoff as their leader, feeling he had the qualities then required to lead Malta and the party in thei
confrontation with Britain over Malta's rights. The Labour Party dubbed its new leader the 'Saviour of Malta' and th
lead to the phrase 'Is-Salvatur ta' Malta'.

   But in the 1950 election the Nationalists gained the most votes and Mintoff became the Leader of the Oppositio
between 1950 and 1954. In 1955, however, the Malta Labour Party led by Dom Mintoff gained a clear majorit
Discussions regarding integration with the United Kingdom were held but relations became strained and in April 195
Mintoff resigned. In the débâcle that followed in 1959 the constitution was again suspended and was not reinstated unt
1962. Mintoff was the prime mover in making Malta a republic and concluded the seven-year agreement with Grea
Britain which included provision for the end of stationing British forces in Malta. Dom Mintoff won the general election
held in 1971 and 1976 and was again sworn in as Prime Minister on 18 December 1981.

CHAPTER FOUR

FEASTS & ENTERTAINMENT

The greasy pole event, known as the giostra, is popular in towns bordering the sea and takes place during the festa of the parish's patron saint. The pole is a tapering mast tied horizontally to the stern of a barge with a red and white flag at the end. The mast is made slippery with grease and soap and youths try to run up it to seize the flag. Most competitors end up in the water!

The Maltese Islands have a rich folklore. Typical of these traditions are the talismans on the bows of fishing boats, those ever-seeing eyes that guard against the dangers of the deep, and there are also the wayside shrines and the stone crosses built into the rubble walls bounding the fields. All have evolved over the past four centuries, along with other numerous beliefs and customs that punctuate the routine of daily life.

There is an important musical tradition in the islands too. 'Il-Maltija', though considered a country dance, probably originated as a court dance in the eighteenth century. Ballad compositions marking sensational happenings – murders and so on – were a thriving art. Unfortunately for many years much of Malta's traditional music fell from favour because it was more lucrative for musicians to join a jazz band, for example, than to preserve the national heritage. However, the popularity of our native culture is now once again increasing. Carnival and the village festa are the two main events in the Maltese calendar. Carnival is held in the run up to Lent; in times gone by the prospect of a period of fasting and penitence in the days before Easter was a great excuse for revelry. When the Order of St John ruled the island some Grand Masters permitted Carnival intemperance, but others regulated it to stamp out rowdy behaviour. The tradition of wearing masks for carnival may have started at this time; the Knights, who were forbidden to participate in the Carnival events, probably used masks to disguise themselves so they could join the festivities. By the twentieth century Valletta Carnival was organized by the British governors and had become the domain of the upper classes, while Nadur, Gozo, was the venue for festivities for the lower classes. This distinction has long ceased to exist. Public Carnival activities in Valletta are now organized by a national committee that also judges the competitions for best floats, costumes and dancing on the square where seating for the public is erected. Processions tend to have a humorous or critical theme. To quote an old saying, '*ogni scherzo vale*' – 'anything is possible'!

Many other celebrations take place during Holy Week. On Good Friday afternoon solemnity and pageantry predominate in the Passion processions held all over the island. The level of participation in the events over the Easter period is remarkable; traditions are faithfully observed. Then summer is ushered in by the Harvest Festival Night, known as Mnarja, on 29 June in the historic Boschetto gardens. The summer calendar continues with numerous festas in honour of each village's patron saint and characterized by street decorations, marching brass bands, recitals and colourful firework displays. For each festa the village church is resplendent with treasures all brought out especially for the occasion. The climax of the celebrations is the procession carrying the statue of the community's patron saint.

On the first weekend in September the two bitterly fought sieges of 1565 and 1940/3 are remembered. A centuries-old regatta is held in the Grand Harbour and it is one of the most popular events of the year.

The calendar pages are punctuated with many other social and cultural activities, sports and pastimes – including Malta's National Day on 31 March. All come together to make up an inheritance that reflects the island's unique character, moulded by the various civilizations that have occupied it over the centuries.

The 'Dutch Skaters' showing off their dance, winning first prize for the best costume at the festa, February 1948.

The Nicolo Isouard Band of Mosta playing at Zebbug's festa of St Philip, *c.* 1960.

Festival of St Joseph, Msida, *c.* 1955.

MANOEL THEATRE

Various sources claim that the Manoel Theatre is the third oldest theatre in Europe. In 1731 Grand Master Manoel de Vilhena wished to erect a theatre 'for the honest recreation of the people', as the Latin inscription above the door still says. He purchased two houses from the Priory of Navarre and work on converting them began immediately. It was originally called the Public Theatre, then became the Theatre Royal, and it was renamed in memory of its founder in 1866.

Its simple, unassuming façade contrasts strongly with its baroque interior, 22-carat gilding and beautifully painted panels representing Mediterranean scenes, musical instruments and laurel leaves. The splendidly ornate royal box was once graced by the Grand Masters of the Order of St John.

The theatre opened its doors on 19 January 1732 and the first production was of the celebrated tragedy *Merope* by Scipione Mattei, acted by the Knights of the Italian Langue. It was followed by two comedies performed on 21 and 26 January and by the French and Italian Knights respectively. The performance of comedies and tragedies by the Knights of St John continued until the order's expulsion from the island in 1777.

The theatre fell quiet during the days of the French occupation but came to life again under the British. There were nights of splendour like 4 December 1838, when Queen Adelaide came with a guard of honour to the performance of *Lucia di Lamermoor*. But by the late nineteenth century the Manoel Theatre had become a victim of its own success and could no longer accommodate the audiences who flocked there. The Royal Opera House was built in 1866 with the proceeds of the sale of the Manoel Theatre. However, it is an ill wind that blows nobody any good . . . . In 1873 the Royal Opera House was destroyed by fire and the opera returned to the Manoel Theatre until the Opera House was rebuilt. The 'little place' in Theatre Street was now on its deathbed and served fitfully as a dance hall before becoming a cinema in the early twentieth century.

In April 1942, during the Second World War, the Royal Opera House was heavily bombed; it was never rebuilt and the lack of an opera venue prompted the revival of the Manoel. The Maltese government listened to the demands of the people and re-acquired the building. Experts from Britain and Italy were appointed to carry out a thorough restoration and decoration programme. The renovation of the theatre was carried out primarily under foreign supervision by Maltese artisans and was completed in fourteen months.

The theatre reopened its doors on 27 December 1960 with a performance of *Coppelia* by the distinguished Ballet Rambert. It became the centre of cultural activities not only for local artists but also for distinguished foreign visitors. Salvatore Accordo, Walter Blankenheim, Siegfried Behrend, Carlos Bonell, Leon Goossens, Vladimir Ashkenazy, Alisio Diaz, Louis Kentner, Yehudi Menuhin and John Ogden are among the many famous performers to have graced the stage.

The Manoel is now officially Malta's national theatre and has its own resident orchestra.

The interior of the Manoel Theatre in the 1990s.

Royal performance, 15 November 1967. The façade of the Manoel Theatre was floodlit and the boxes were decorated with red and white carnations and green laurel garlands. A burst of applause greeted Queen Elizabeth II, beautifully striking in a classic white gown accentuated by the glitter of diamonds and rubies. The 'National Anthem' was played and then the Chorus Melitensis sang a religious work accompanied by the orchestra. This was followed by Poulenc's 'Concerto for Piano and Orchestra' and Rimsky-Korsakov's 'La Grande Pasque Russe'.

The New York Harp Ensemble at the Manoel Theatre, 12 April 1983. The ensemble played at many presidential palaces and were invited to perform at the White House by President Ronald Reagan.

Performances

AT THE

Manoel Theatre

VALLETTA — MALTA

Grand Opening Night

on TUESDAY, 27th DECEMBER, 1960, at 8.15 p.m

COPPELIA

A Ballet by Saint Leon — Music by Delibes

Wednesday, 28th December, 1960, at 8.30 p.m.

Repeat Performance of "COPPELIA".

GALA NIGHT on THURSDAY, 29th DECEMBER, 1960

GISELLE AND CZERNY...ANA

By Adam   *By Czerny*

Friday, 30th December, 1960, at 8.30 p.m.

Repeat Performance of "GISELLE" and "CZERNY ... ANA"

A page from the programme for the Ballet Rambert's performances of *Coppelia* which marked the re-opening of the Manoel Theatre, 27 December 1960.

MANOEL THEATRE
GRAND OPERA SEASON 1961.
Impresa Ines Cantoni
Repertoire'

NORMA	FEDORA	ZAZA'
Vincenzo Bellini	*Umberto Giordano*	*Ruggiero Leoncavallo*

IL BARBIERE DI SIVIGLIA
Gioacchino Rossini

LA BOHEME	RIGOLETTO
Giacomo Puccini	*Giuseppe Verdi*

LIST OF ARTISTS (*In Alphabetical Order*)

LADIES: LUCIANA BERTOLLI - ARMANDA BONATO
DARIA DANISE - CARLA FERRARIO
MARGHERITA GUGLIELMI - JOLANDA MONGELLI
MIETTA SIGHELE - ADRIANA TURRINI.

GENTLEMEN: ROBERT KELLER - ALFONSO MARCHICA
VELLO MANFRIN - AFRO POLI
LORENZO SABATUCCI - FELICE SCHIAVI
GIUSEPPE SAVIO - PIERO SCACCIATI
OTTAVIO SERPO - IGINIO VALSECCHI
GIUSEPPE VICENTINI.

ORCHESTRA CONDUCTORS
GIUSEPPE MORELLI — TINO CREMAGNIANI
PRODUCER
Comm. AUGUSTO CARDI
ASSISTANT CONDUCTOR
AMELIO REGOLIN
PROMPTER
GIACINTO POLONI
CHORUS MASTERS
ERNESTO PIRISI — J. ABELA SCOLARO
LEADING VIOLINIST
GIORLANDO VALENTE

Light Effects: CHARLES TABONE   Dressmaking: M.A. CAMILLERI.
Hairdresser: TONY GALEA   Costumes: M.A. CAMILLERI-ARDOVINO.
Scenery: SORMANI   Footwear: PEDRAZZOLI   Wigs: FOURLAI.
Furniture: Messrs. Gio. BATTA DELIA   Lighting: PALAZZO della LUCE.

A page from the programme for Impresa Cantoni's début at the Manoel Theatre in Bellini's opera *Norma*, January 1961.

A soloist performing the dance of the dying swan from *Swan Lake*, c. 1937.

The Chamber Opera Lubeck (Konzertante Kammeroper Lubeck), an ensemble of singers and instrumentalists founded by and under the direction of Gisela Jahn, presented Alessandro Scarlatti's 'Il Giardino di Rosa' at the Manoel Theatre on 28 October 1971.

The Manoel Theatre Academy of Dramatic Art (MTADA) presented *Jubilee and Black Comedy* at the Manoel Theatre on 15 December 1977, during the international arts festival. In the centre of the picture is Emanuel Scicluna who at one time held the position of theatre manager. The actress is Josette Ciappara who is now a director and producer of plays at the theatre. MTADA runs study programmes at both junior and senior levels in voice techniques, movement, interpretation, improvisation, rehearsal and stage management.

Malta - Valletta - The Opera House

The Royal Opera House. In 1863 this was the *Illustrated London News*'s description of the building: 'It is in the Italian style of architecture, having a handsome portico supported by four columns of the Corinthian order, approached from a bold terrace by a flight of steps, the terrace itself having two approaches by steps at each end. The base of the building restricted and ornamented with four lions *couchant*.' This once magnificent building was completed in 1866 at a cost of more than £25,000 and was designed by E.M. Barry, the architect of the Royal Opera House in Covent Garden, London. It opened on 28 March with a performance of Bellini's *I Puritani*.

Just over seven years later disaster struck. On Sunday 25 May 1873 the final rehearsal for *La Vergine del Castello*, a new opera by Privitera, was taking place. During the third act the alarm was raised – the stage was on fire. The building was evacuated and in the hours that followed its interior was engulfed by flames. A powder magazine was known to be close by and thousands of people fled the town in fear of an explosion. Fortunately, their fears were unfounded.

Raising funds for the repairs was difficult. Eventually the Council agreed to fund the restoration and on 26 May 1875 a sum of £12,000 was voted for that purpose. The restoration was completed in two years and the new Opera House was inaugurated on 11 October 1877 with a performance of Verdi's *Aida*.

On the evening of 7 April 1942, during the large-scale German bombing of Valletta, the Royal Opera House was hit. As the *Times of Malta* said, 'like the Pantheon, the Royal Opera House harks back to a glorious age. As it stands in ruins, it highlights a symbol of high culture and the glorious age Malta has lost.'

he Royal Opera House on fire, 25 May 1873. This photograph was taken from the Picket House on Porta Reale. For four ears the Opera House was unable to host productions because of the extensive fire damage.

oyal Opera House, 1942. Valletta's pride and joy was reduced to a heap of rubble after direct hits by German high xplosive bombs on 7 April 1942.

The interior of the Royal Opera House, *c*. 1935.

A performance of the ballet *Sylphides* by Princess Poutiatine at the Royal Opera House ballet school, 1936.

Princess Poutiatine at the final curtain call for *The Dance of the Flowers, c.* 1935. Russian-born Princess Nathalie Poutiatine pioneered the teaching of classical ballet in Malta in the late 1920s. She was born in St Petersburg and was given her first ballet lessons by Madame Tamara Karasavina. The Bolshevik revolution of 1917 forced the Poutiatine family to leave their homeland and settle in Paris. Nathalie began ballet lessons taught by professional Russian teachers. She was then auditioned by the great Anna Pavlova who promised Nathalie a place in her ballet company. Princess Poutiatine married a Maltese, Edgar Tabone, and founded the first classical ballet school on the island.

The Princess Poutiatine ballet school, *c.* 1934. Students in this picture include Joy Micallef Eynaud, Yvonne Muscat, Iris Merola and Irene Cox. The pianist is Rose Critien.

Maltese-born Paul Asciak as Otello (right) and Piero Cappuccilli as Iago in Verdi's *Otello* at the Argotti Gardens, Floriana. The opera was performed by the Milanese company Impressa Cantoni as part of the St Paul's Shipwreck Celebrations in 1960. Paul Asciak's operatic career lasted from 1946 to 1961. Following concerts with the world-famous singers Tito Schipa and Maria Caniglia, and encouraged by the latter, he went to Rome where he studied mainly under Alberto Paoletti and Luigi Ricci at the Teatro dell'Opera. In 1951 he won the Spoleto Concorso when he sang Radames in *Aida*. He performed at the Royal Opera House in Covent Garden, London, in 1952, appearing in various roles. For further information see *The Making of a Maltese Tenor* by V.M. Pellegrini (1989).

Tito Gobbi (left) being entertained at the Phoenicia Hotel after a performance, May 1947. The author is standing on the right. Gobbi, one of the twentieth century's greatest baritones, was born on 24 October 1913 and studied with tenor Giulio Crimi, gaining a contract with La Scala in Milan as early as 1935. In 1947, when he visited Malta, he was poised on the edge of a major international career. In 1951 he came to the island again, this time to sing in some of Verdi's operas at the Knights' Hall Theatre. In the same year he began his long professional association with Maria Callas.

was a custom among Maltese families to put children in
ncy dress during Carnival, *c.* 1930.

he Ghawazi Group representing an Arab tribe, Main Guard Square, Valletta, Carnival of 1930.

The Evzones winning first prize in the Carnival dancing competition, 1947.

The Toy Soldiers winning second prize for their float at the Carnival, 1948.

Carnival float with the theme 'Wee Bonnie Scots', by the Salvu Bonnello Co., 1968. The float was designed to look like a Scottish castle and children danced to Scottish songs and ballads.

Carnival float by the Salvu Bonnello Co., 1969. The float (left) was based on the story of Pinocchio. When the float reached the Main Guard Square, children interpreted the tales in dance (below).

Children dressed as the 'Antennae Species from Pluto' in the Carnival 1970. They joined the parade into Valletta in their very own flying saucer!

Carnival float by the Salvu Bonnello Co., Senglea, 1972. This large float had 'Maltese Souvenirs' as its theme. Some of the children on it were dressed in 'Faldetta' Maltese lace, others had costumes representing peasants and nobles. A cannon was a reminder of the 1565 siege and other features included a village festa and Imnarja. After the procession the children danced to folk music in the Main Guard Square, Valletta.

...he sandy beach of Armier Bay,
...1920.

Watersports near The Tower,
Sliema, *c.* 1920.

...thing beauties in 1922 —
...s time the three are without
...ince the Pomeranian
...e p. 93).

The presentation of colours to the Royal Malta Regiment in front of St John's cathedral, 1 January 1895.

The presentation of two royal banners to the Prince of Wales' Own Band Club in Neptune's Courtyard, the Palace Valletta, 18 March 1901. A bronze statue of Neptune stands in the courtyard. Formerly it was at the centre of the fish market in front of Ta'Liesse church, Marima.

Nicolo Isouard Band Club committee, October 1911. When Napoleon departed Malta on 19 June 1798 he left General Vaubois in command and one of Vaubois's first acts was to appoint Nicolo Isouard as Commissioner of the Manoel Theatre (*see* p. 110). He was also an organist and later Maestro Di Capella at St John's cathedral. Isouard composed many pieces of sacred music and his operas were performed all over Europe. The large library of the Nicolo Isouard Band Club holds volumes of his work and his music is regularly performed.

The Duke of Edinburgh's Band after a performance of Puccini's *Tosca* at the Royal Opera House, 1918. The band was established in Vittoriosa in 1858 but was not given its title until 1891 when there was a substantial British naval presence in Malta. It obtained patronage from Prince Alfred, Duke of Edinburgh, which gave members the right to wear uniforms similar to his military one. In 1892 the band welcomed the Prince on his arrival in Malta on HMS *Surprise*. They became the guest band of the Admiralty, performing every Friday at naval establishments. In 1978 the band was renamed the St Lawrence Band Club of Vittoriosa but retains the patronage of Prince Philip, Duke of Edinburgh.

The Prince of Wales' Own Band Club of Birgu. The band was formed on 27 September 1891 under the name ‹
Vittoriosa Philharmonic Society. In 1895 it obtained the patronage of the Duke of York and became known as the Duke ‹
York's Own. The band took part in religious feasts, national celebrations and played funeral marches. The arrival of th
Duke and Duchess of York at the Customs House on 25 March 1901 was marked by the band playing 'God Save th
King'. When the Duke was created Prince of Wales on the death of Queen Victoria he gave his consent to change th
band's name to Prince of Wales' Own Band and on 26 December 1903 Governor Sir Charles Mansfield Clarke, presente
members with a new standard. It retains the name to this day in honour of the present Prince of Wales.

Decorations and celebrations in Mosta Street on 15 August to
mark the feast of Santa Maria, early twentieth century.

endi men carrying fireworks to be used to celebrate the festa of the village's patron saint, *c.* 1960.

ish priest Father Kalcedon Schembri blesses the Melita Band on the parvis of Msida church, 10 December 1922. Note two ferry landing piers in the background.

La Stella Band committee, Gudja, 1921/2. Back row, left to right: A. Caruana, G. Gatt, A. Agius. Middle row: G. Baldacchino, E. Micallef, G. Dalli, G. Pace. Front row: L. Caruana, C. Zammit, G. Galdes, A. Dalli, Gio Abdilla.

La Stella Band, March 1951. During the British era governors made a habit of visiting band clubs in the villages and towns around the island as part of their attempts to foster good relations with the Maltese. Band clubs had far wider significance than just playing music: after the parish church, they were the most important institution in a community and brought people together. Many clubs played host to royalty and celebrities.

Birgu parochial committee for the organization of the seventh centenary festivities commemorating the death of St Dominic, 1922.

Birkirkara traces its origins back to the Middle Ages. The first parish church was dedicated to the Assumption of the Virgin and was built in the Renaissance style at the beginning of the seventeenth century. Around 100 years later a larger church in the baroque style was erected and dedicated to St Helena. The younger church has twin belfries and seven bells in all, the largest and latest of which (right) was cast in Milan and hoisted into place in 1932. It is the biggest bell in Malta and the third largest in the world. The parish also has an important reminder of Malta's past — its windmill. This was one of several built across the island and it was still working at the beginning of the twentieth century. However, much has changed in Birkirkara in recent decades. The ancient terraced fields, with their characteristic rubble walls, and the centenarian carob trees have now given way to new factories.

Eucharistic Congress, 1913. On 24 April after a rally at the Floriana granaries, the children attending the Catechism of Porto Salvo, proceeded to Valletta led by Auxiliary Bishop Angelo Portell OP to be greeted by Cardinal Domenico Ferrata in Queens Square. The children in their first communion clothes were preceded by the effigy of Our Lady of the Holy Rosary.

Malta is the only country in the British Commonwealth to have featured the Virgin Mother on its stamps. The 1951 series commemorated the seventh centenary of the Carmelite Scapular and showed Our Lady bestowing the scapular (or cloak) on the English saint Simon Stock.

ocession of Christ arisen, Cospicua, Easter Sunday
orning, c. 1950. The statue is raced up the stairs of the
urch as a symbol of the ascension. Many Maltese
ditions centre around Easter. Another takes place on
od Friday when some people join the main procession
agging chains. The custom dates back to the time when
e Knights began the tradition of walking through the
eets to commemorate Easter and insisted that the
archers include slaves who were shackled during the
ocession.

A votive procession from Birkirkara to Cospicua, 1944. As
air raids abated the parishioners brought the image of the
Immaculate Conception back to the village.

Boy Scouts marking the feast of St George, their patron saint, with a march past. His Excellency Sir Maurice Dorman, t
last Governor-General of Malta, took the salute and was accompanied by Lady Dorman, the Vicar-General Monsign
E. Galea and the island Commissioner E.J. Cuschieri.

Msida Boy Scouts investiture ceremony, *c.* 1930. Group Scoutmaster Wilfred Rizzo invests Joe Grixti as a Rover.

CHAPTER FIVE

TRANSPORT, COMMERCE, FISHING & FARMING

The interior of a public bar, a place for relaxation after a hard day's work in the dockyards, c. 1935. Notice the sign for 'Hot Rum'. Navy rum was mixed with water and poured into a glass then a poker was heated in a brazier, had the ash knocked off it and was thrust into the mixture. This process was repeated in many bars frequented by British naval personnel who also enjoyed fine Maltese beer, brewed on the island by Farsons (see pp. 136–9).

THE RAILWAY

Malta railway was inaugurated on 28 February 1883 amid scenes of great celebration: so began the working life of the railway that ran seven trains daily from Valletta to Notabile and back. It was later extended to Mtarfa, stopping at Floriana, Hamrun, Msida, St Venera, Birkirkara, Balzan, San Anton, Attard, San Salvatore and Rabat. The trains would run more frequently and with more coaches during festas and special events.

Originally it was intended to construct a network of lines covering practically the whole island but the project was largely abandoned. Only the extension to Mtarfa was added to the original line; the government purchased six new engines and put down lines to reach the military garrisons in Mtarfa from where a large number of troops bought 7d tickets to travel down to the 'fleshpots' of Valletta. All engines running the line were 'Tank' class, dark olive green in colour with black smoke boxes and vermilion buffer beams. The brass domes and chimneys had copper bands at the top. The wheels and frames were black and each engine carried a brass oval number plate. Carriages were four-wheeled wooden vehicles with steel chassis and had seats along their entire length so that people sat facing one another. Until 1900 the trains were lit by candles; paraffin oil lamps were fitted later, except for in the Governor's carriages which had electric lights run from accumulators charged by a dynamo that was worked by a belt from one of the axles.

Strange accidents occurred on the railway. For example, on 22 July 1923 a ship had brought in a load of bullocks that were landed at pens in St Venera. They were herded to a level-crossing. Unfortunately the barrier was down but the bullocks pressed against it and went on to the railway track. The train driver could not stop the train on time and it crashed into the herd. No one on board was injured but a few of the bullocks were killed.

Railway repairs and renovations to the trains were done in the dockyard at first but by 1900 Hamrun station housed an engineering headquarters, workshops and even a small foundry. The staff manning the trains were well dressed in their navy blue uniforms with shiny brass buttons and conductors were renowned for their decorum and authority! But by 1905 the railway's heyday was over. The first blow to the popularity of the trains came when Malta's tramway system opened in 1905. Passengers preferred the new means of transport and the railway rapidly lost business, declined and closed on 31 March 1931. The railway tunnel came to life again during the Second World War, however. It was cleared of debris, bunk beds were installed and it was used as an air-raid shelter and a refuge for the homeless.

Attard station, on the Valletta to Mtarfa railway, c. 1910.

The Malta railway terminus at Porta Reale, *c.* 1920.

Employees of the Malta Railway Co. Ltd pose with engine no. 5 at Museum station, Mdina, 1920.

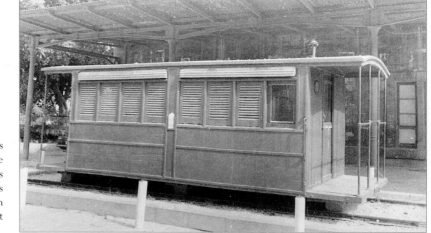

This third-class carriage has survived, minus its chassis, axle and wheels, since 1931. It was probably originally a first-class carriage and has now been restored for exhibition at Birkirkara station.

FARSONS BREWERY

Farsons is one of the oldest leading firms in Malta. Established in the late 1920s at Hamrun by Henry and George Simonds and the Farrugia brothers, it has prospered and outgrown its original premises.

The Simonds' connection with Malta began in 1875. They read a report on the strength of the British garrisons on the island and saw a significant business opportunity. A Malta branch of the brewery business was established by 1890 with an office in Valletta and stores in Marsa. The latter were strategically placed to receive bulk beer deliveries landed from barges that were then transferred on to horse-drawn carts to be carried inland. This was a lucrative business at a time when sailors' bars lined the harbour fronts and narrow streets of Valletta, Floriana, Senglea and Sliema.

The Simonds merged their interests with the Farrugia brothers and created Simonds Farsons Ltd, brewers. An all-out marketing campaign then began. Groups from Farsons went to every outlet where beer was sold promoting the brew. Contracts were made with the service messes and the NAAFI and Farsons took over the running of the buffet at the Royal Opera House in Valletta.

The company also started exporting beer, particularly to the Maltese communities in North Africa, and its 'Blue Label' was a popular brand in Egypt and Palestine. In the 1930s, when the political situation in the Mediterranean became uncertain, these regular deliveries were threatened. However, in spite of international tension, Farsons fulfilled its commitments to the NAAFI and continued to deliver thousands of cases of beer to British troops in Egypt and Ismalia.

But in June 1940, when Italy joined the Second World War, Malta was declared a danger zone. Simonds Farsons left the offices in the Strada Reale. Later a new brewery on a grand scale was built at Mriehel. The expansion plans included installing a vast boiling copper nearly 14 ft in diameter and weighing 10 tons. It arrived by ship at Marsa and a trailer had to be hired from the Air Ministry to transport it to the new brewery.

The company continued trading until 1948 when it was wound up, only to reopen the next day as Simonds Farsons Cisk Ltd. In the decade that followed it achieved renown all over the world.

A convoy of lorries carrying Farsons products, c. 1950.

Above: The Valletta offices of H. & G. Simonds on the ground floor of the Palazzo Ferreria, 1890. *Right*: Rose & Crown, a popular Navy bar in St Julian's, 1930s.

Officers of H. & G. Simonds outside the firm's headquarters, Valletta, 1890.

Simonds Farsons Cisk Ltd, 1950. Left to right: Archbishop Monsignor M. Gonzi, Brigadier Simonds de Brett, His Excellency Sir Gerald Creasey (Governor) Mr Edward Farrugia, Mr L.V. Farrugia, Mr W. Harding, Mr J. Cachia and Mrs L.V. Farrugia.

SIMONDS'

CELEBRATED

A L E S & S T O U T
SOLD EVERYWHERE

The Brewery, Reading,

ENGLAND

OVER 100 YEARS' REPUTATION !
MALTA BRANCH, 611 SRADA REALE

'BLUE LABEL' Ale

PURITY   QUALITY

THE BEST AND MOST POPULAR BEER.

Awarded the Certificate of
the Institute of Hygiene,
London, for Purity and
Quality.

Refuse substitutes by having
the bottle opened before you

SIMONDS - FARSONS, LTD.
THE BREWERY, MALTA.

Above: Advertisement from the *Il Currier Malti*, 4 April 1908. *Right*: Advertisement from the *Malta Chronicle*, 12 November 1934.

A foot-pedal operated Crown Cork machine, manufactured in England and used in the early days at Farsons.

Women at work in Farsons brewery, 1950s.

Loading Farsons products for shipment to North Africa, 1940s.

MARSOVIN

A convoy of lorries from the Marsovin winery. Malta has an ancient association with viticulture but owes its real revival since Roman times to the Knights of St John. More recently the production of wine has increased dramatically. In the last 100 years three generations of the Cassar family have made the name Marsovin the standard bearer for quality Maltese wine. Wine drinking has become established as an important part of the islands' culture.

Baskets of grapes from the Marsovin factory. Antony Cassar, who founded the factory in 1919, used a cart to deliver the barrels. Running on wheels almost as tall as a man, the horse-drawn vehicles took supplies all over the island. The wine pump used to transfer the liquid to the barrels was operated by hand.

Sturdy locally made devices, including presses and pumps, were used on the island (above). An assortment of scales and chains was traditionally used to determine the weight of containers of grapes (below). A basket of grapes was suspended from the hook at the end of the chain and its weight would be indicated on the special graduated ruler by the counterweight. Nowadays modern pressing plants, cellars and bottling factories have been built and equipped with the technology to develop the latest scientific techniques for wine production. Baskets of grapes – both grown locally and imported – are processed as soon as they reach the winery.

MANOEL ISLAND

Manoel Island slipways, Gzira, *c.* 1970. Manoel de Vilhena, the Portuguese Grand Master of the Order of St John, built a larg[e] fort on an islet in Marsamxetto Harbour. The foundation stone was laid on 14 September 1723 and the fort was completed [in] 1732. It had a garrison of 500 men to guard against invasion and the fort and island both took the name of the Gran[d] Master.

Yachts tied to the jetty for repairs, *c.* 1970. Nearby Fort Manoel is in the shape of a square with four corner bastions, a wide ditc[h] and a north side reinforced against the most likely direction of attack. Inside there is a parade ground and three barrack buildings.

Manoel Island yacht yard, 1969. Monsignor Emanuel Gerad is visiting the island's slipways accompanied by the yard's management. The tradition of boatbuilding on Manoel Island goes back to the days of the Order of St John. Nelson's ships were also repaired here and the craftsmen serviced British naval vessels during the nineteenth and early twentieth centuries.

Workmen at Manoel Island yacht yard, c. 1970. During the Second World War the island was the base for naval barges. After 1945 the modernization of the slips and the provision of berthing facilities on the island became part of Malta's dockyard development programme. Since its conversion to the construction of yachts in 1966 the yard has handled all manner of vessels and exhibited boats at the International Boat Show at Earls Court in London.

The cargo boat *Ta'Latina* is hauled down Marsa slipway, *c*. 1960. The greased beams on the slipway enable the boat to move smoothly into the water.

Manning the slipway, *c*. 1960.

Chadwick lakes, *c*. 1950. These were built in the days of Lord Chadwick, Governor of Malta.

Barges laden with coal arrived almost daily at Ta'Xbiex wharf in the 1930s. Their consignments were unloaded, stored in yards and distributed to fuel the island's industries.

Royal Navy floating dock with Valletta on the left and St Angelo on the right, *c.* 1950.

The Gozo–Malta boat *Imperial Eagle*, 1961. Doris Cassar is standing on the foreshore.

The *Imperial Eagle* arriving at Mtarfa, 1961.

Solemar Hotel, Mtarfa landing stage, April 1961. The hotel has since been demolished.

A Maltese calesse, late nineteenth century.

Working at St Andrew's barracks during the Second World War. Left to right: Louis, Albert, Manuel and Joe Sammut.

A cab or karozzin built by Giuseppe Micallef, *c.* 1930.

A 1920s bus. Before being converted to carry passengers this vehicle was used by the British authorities as an ambulance. It was built by Joe Micallef of Msida.

The first Ford in Malta, bought by Joseph Muscat, *c.* 1927.

This bus turned over at a crucial point on Ghadira Hill, *c.* 1960.

Look around you and count the number of

Morris, Wolseleys & M G Cars

that are filling the roads.
YOUR NEXT MOVE

question the owners themselves, they cannot mis-
lead you because there is no reason whatever in
doing this.

They will tell you that **MORRIS PRODUCT** has
given them 100% satisfaction in all directions.

And this cannot fail, because Morris Products are
build on the **SPECIALISATION** Process involving
555 inspection process on the 1556 component
part of a 16 h.p. engine.

ELEGANCE-ECONOMY-APPEARANCE-PERFORMANCE

"MORRIS" THE 100 % BRITISH CAR

	MIZZI BROTHERS
Tel. 1118.	**SOLE DISTRIBUTORS**
	283, Sda: Reale, Valletta.

1937 advertisement for the Morris car.

A seven-seater Buick. One of the earliest cars imported
to Malta, this vehicle was owned by Joseph Muscat.

A Maltese farmer harvesting during an air raid in the early 1940s.

Potato picking, 1960. Farming is still almost entirely a family concern: men, women and children all work on the land and little or no outside labour is employed. Farm holdings were once very small and did not lend themselves to being worked by machinery, but there are now large, levelled fields that need to be ploughed by tractors. In 1943 the Department of Agriculture introduced threshing machines and these are now popular. The old practice was to have a threshing floor where the grain was trodden down by donkeys, cows or mules and winnowed by being tossed into the air — the wind blew the chaff away (*see* p. 151).

...hreshing floor, *c*. 1935. The ground is levelled by chipping off the rocks and adding a layer of soil. Donkeys then trample ... flat by walking round and round.

1937 advertisement for the Hygienic Alimentary ...ste Factory.

Working in the fields, *c*. 1930. A farmer and his two cows plough with the Verdala Palace in the background.

Potato picking behind a wooden plough, *c.* 1950.

A donkey pulling a cart loaded with sacks of fertilizer crosses a police barrier, *c.* 1950

Laying nets on the wharf for mending at Marsaxlokk, *c.* 1960. This village was the point at which Turkish forces landed to mount their invasion of Malta in 1565. Napoleon's troops also came ashore here in 1798. Marsaxlokk is renowned for its fish market and its harbour is home to the island's largest fishing fleet.

Unloading fish from a government vessel, *c.* 1960. Some twenty motor boats, ranging in length from 20 to 79 feet, and 620 smaller vessels are currently engaged in fishing off Malta. There are two main fishing seasons: mackerel is caught from May to September; corephene (lampuki) and pilot fish (fanfri) are landed from August to November. From December to April rough seas confine the boats to harbour.

A watering cart is replenished with sea water ready to spray the streets to keep the dust down, Spinola Bay, St Julian's, early twentieth century.

Until the beginning of the Second World War Bertu Aquilina made his own wine from grapes grown on his property in St Andrew's. Any wine that went sour was poured into the 'darminggjan' – a large glass bottle – and left on the roof to ferment (above) into vinegar for domestic use.

A boy selling milk from his goat, c. 1920. Coffee sho sometimes kept a goat tied up by the entrance to enti clients in with the promise of fresh milk.

Maltese goats, *c.* 1950.

A mule driving a flour mill. Since time immemorial horses, mules and donkeys have been helping man in the fields. Ploughing was done by a beast muzzled to stop him nibbling. Mules were also used to trample harvested sheaves on the threshing floor. Farmers took wheat to the mill to be ground and this work was also done by donkeys and mules; they turned the wheels that ground wheat into flour. The mule would be blindfolded for this work so it would not get dizzy.

Traditional Maltese hand-woven cloth was once always in demand. In the days of sail, Maltese sailcloth was market
throughout the Mediterranean and was known for its excellent quality. Malta weave was also used for clothing and f
house furnishings. These women were photographed in about 1920.

Maltese lace has established a reputation for its delicacy and
quality. Its origins can be traced back to about 1640 when it was
used mainly to decorate churches. Our mothers and
grandmothers adorned their dowry with lace made to intricate
designs. This picture dates from about 1930.

Woman hawkers sold eggs and all kinds of oth
products, from vegetables to medicinal herbs a
canework baskets, from door to door. This illustrat
is from about 1910.

-Ballata. Up to the Second World War, before the general
se of concrete, women beaters were employed to beat
oofs flat. They used to beat the mixture of fragments of
ottery and lime on the roof with a flat wooden block and
vorked in twos or threes in a row, backwards from one
nd of the roof to the other. They worked long hours and
vere poorly paid.

Cloth sellers at Pieta Creek, *c.* 1930.

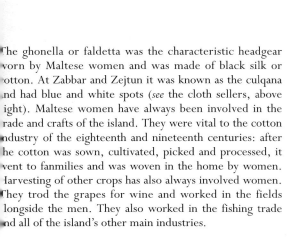

he ghonella or faldetta was the characteristic headgear
vorn by Maltese women and was made of black silk or
otton. At Zabbar and Zejtun it was known as the culqana
nd had blue and white spots (*see* the cloth sellers, above
ight). Maltese women have always been involved in the
rade and crafts of the island. They were vital to the cotton
ndustry of the eighteenth and nineteenth centuries: after
he cotton was sown, cultivated, picked and processed, it
vent to fanmilies and was woven in the home by women.
Harvesting of other crops has also always involved women.
They trod the grapes for wine and worked in the fields
longside the men. They also worked in the fishing trade
nd all of the island's other main industries.

The arrival of a British Airways flight at the old Luqa airport, 1970s. Visitors from all over the world now come to Malta or holiday.

THROUGH THE PAST AND ON INTO THE FUTURE

On 1 April 1974 a new page in Malta's history was turned when the first two aircraft on lease to Air Malta took off from Luqa airport and provided a new link between the island and the rest of Europe, making this corner of the Mediterranean more accessible to travellers.

Since then Malta has welcomed many thousands of tourists, attracted by the history and vibrancy of these remarkable islands. Open-air events are staged every year to celebrate Malta's culture and heritage and range from full-scale military parades to re-enactments of historic events. Tourists are welcomed into the islands' myriad villages and are introduced to the people's traditional way of life. The visitor is guaranteed to go home happy, having spent a holiday on an enchanting group of islands.

ACKNOWLEDGEMENTS

I record my grateful thanks to the following. I apologise if a name or a reference has been omitted through an oversight:

Anglo-Maltese Band Club • Mary Aquilina • Paul Asciak • Reno Attard Montalto • Salv. Bonello Frances Bonnici • Paul Borg • John Brincat • Fr Joseph Calleja • Edward Cassar • Joseph Cauchi Raymond Cauchi • Judge M. Caruana Curran • Josette Ciantar • Pauline Debono • Din l-Art Helwa • Duke of Edinburgh's Band Club • Fr Edgar of the Jesuits, Zejtun • Irina Farrugia Farsons Ltd • Kate Flattery • Marguerite Fuller • Dr Sylvia Haslam • Marianne Hogen Information Department • The Squire de Lisle • Len Kilgour • Marsovin Ltd • Sylvana Mifsud Yvonne Mifsud • National War Museum Association • Louis Naudi • Josette Petroni • Josette Portelli • Prince of Wales' Band Club • Queen's Own Band Club • La Stella Band Club • Tony Terrible • *Times of Malta* • Mary Vella • Andy Welsh • Westin Hotel • Brian Wilkes • Lorenzo Zahra • Lydia Zammit • Joanna Zammit Maempel.

I also wish to record my thanks to the many people with whom I have discussed this book and who have given me good advice. I apologise for not listing them all individually.

Jean de La Vallette, elected Grand Master of the Order of St John in 1557, was a great leader, who was as prudent as he was courageous. La Valette, who is always represented as a heroic leader with military genius, was also endowed with great faith. He always invoked God's help and mercy. The building of a new city, the fortification of the Island of Gozo, the sending of Fra Martino Rojas to the Council of Trent, the treaty with Philip II of Spain and the gaining of many rich prizes from enemy shipping, were among his achievements. He had the foresight to stock Malta with provisions and munitions in preparation for the siege launched by the Turkish Sultan Suleiman's army on 19 May 1565; the assault lasted until 8 September and the island survived. The Grand Master often weighed in himself where the fighting was the fiercest and for this he not only received the praise of all the Christian princes but was also presented with a sword and dagger by Philip II. Pope Pius IV offered to make him a cardinal but he humbly refused. Immediately after the siege he started building a city on Mount Sceberras; under the auspices of Pius V the first stone was placed on 28 March 1566 and the finished city was named Valletta. He died in 1568 and was buried in the vault of St John's cathedral.

The author standing on the disused railway track that ran over the stone bridge at Porte des Bombes.

THE AUTHOR

Carmelina Grech was born in Msida in 1924, attended the local primary school and then the secondary school at the Auberge de France, Valletta. She qualified as a civil servant and was posted to the government's treasury department, becoming secretary to the treasurer, the Hon. Edgar Cuschieri OBE. Taking further examinations she qualified for a teacher training degree at Cambridge University, but the war intervened and she was unable to travel to take up her place to study.

She married Edward Grech and raised a family of four boys and one girl while taking on various part-time jobs with the government. In 1960 she was appointed secretary to Michael Kissaun, Manager of the Manoel Theatre. After the birth of her fifth child she worked as secretary to the chief accountant at HM dockyard, eventually transferring to the Manoel Island yacht yard and visiting Earl's Court in London as part of the yard's support staff for an international exhibition.

In 1977 she qualified in journalism at the University of Malta. She retired from full-time employment at the age of sixty but remained involved with philanthropic societies as secretary to the Friends of Manoel Theatre, Treasurer to the National Trust of Malta and Public Relations Officer for the Maltese branch of the International Tree Foundation. In her varied career she has travelled widely, visiting most European countries, Russia, and much of Asia and Australasia.